TAKE DOWN SPANISH FOR LAW ENFORCEMENT

A Road Officer's Guide
Second Edition

Detective Steve W. Gaenzle – Retired

TAKE DOWN SPANISH FOR LAW ENFORCEMENT
A Road Officer's Guide
Second Edition

Copyright © 2018 Steve Gaenzle. All rights reserved. No part of this book may be reproduced or retransmitted in any form or by any means without the written permission of the author.

ISBN – 13: 978-1727864397
ISBN – 10: 1727864397

A Road Officer's Guide – Second Edition

I want to thank all my Spanish teachers over the years. My Spanish speaking partners and most importantly my beautiful wife, Joanne who has supported me through the years of traveling and teaching Spanish to first responders across the country. She has been the inspiration of my teachings and supported me throughout the long hours of sitting behind a computer authoring training materials and text books.

To those who have given their lives in the protection of our great country -

THANK YOU!

AUTHOR BIOGRAPHY
Detective Steve W. Gaenzle - Retired

Steve has 26 years of distinguished service as a peace officer. He has been decorated with the Distinguished Service Medal as well as Meritorious Services to his community. Steve began his career with the El Paso County Sheriff's Office in El Paso, Texas, his hometown. The demand of knowing the Spanish language was paramount in this border town. He instructed in the West-Texas Regional Training Academy in El Paso, Texas and then continued his career in Colorado Springs, Colorado as a Colorado Peace Officer. He has been a field supervisor, Field Training Officer - FTO, undercover detective assigned to the FBI Federal Fugitive Task Force, and a lead homicide detective in a major crimes unit, with numerous high profile murder investigations. Steve has also appeared numerous times in the hit television series, **Homicide Hunter** with Lt. Joe Kenda as shown on the *I*nvestigation *D*iscovery channel.

In addition to being a Spanish language instructor, Steve has instructed Interview and Interrogation, Crime Scene Search and Protection, Law Enforcement Driving Instructor, (EVO), Firearms Instructor and Colorado Criminal Law. Steve has been instrumental in creating new Spanish training programs for dispatchers, patrol, jail and prison personnel , undercover and narcotics officers and created Spanish training programs in Alabama, Arkansas, Colorado, Georgia, Kentucky, Louisiana, Mississippi, Montana, New Mexico, Ohio, Tennessee, Texas, Utah and many other states.

Steve is recognized as an expert in the field of law enforcement for the Spanish language. Steve has been the lead Spanish instructor for the Rocky Mountain High Intensity Drug Trafficking Area, RMHIDTA; the Gulf Coast HIDTA; the Ohio HIDTA and the Spanish instructor for the Regional Counterdrug Training Academy, RCTA, in Meridian, Mississippi. Not only authoring this book, Steve has written <u>Take Down Law Enforcement Spanish</u> – First Edition© and <u>Spanish for the Peace Officer</u>©. Dedication and the love for law enforcement have driven Steve for decades to teach and help first responders across the country. Steve has instructed tens of thousands of law enforcement officers as well as first responders in many fields albeit civilian, sworn peace officers, federal agents and military personnel. Steve is highly sought as a Spanish language instructor and instructor for multiple disciplines across the country.

CONTENT ADVISEMENT

This publication is designed to provide accurate and authoritative information with regard to the subject matter covered. It is marketed and sold with the understanding that the publisher and the author are not engaged in rendering legal, accounting, or other professional advice. If legal advice or other expert assistance is required, the services of a competent professional person should be sought. The author has made every effort to provide up to date information contained within this publication. Caution should be considered when speaking a foreign language, in that, words change meanings throughout regions and different parts of the world. The author cannot be held liable for any acts taken, any words spoken, written, or uttered in any form or fashion by the reader of this text. At no time may any part of this publication be copied, transmitted in any form or used in any manner without the written consent of the author and or Spanish Language Consultants, LLC.

FOREWORD

Welcome my friends "**Bienvenidos mis amigos**." You have begun the absolute best step in becoming a Spanish speaker by opening this book. Over the past four decades, Spanish-speaking people within the United States have grown exponentially. Today, the stress on Law Enforcement personnel, dispatchers, EMTs, Fire Fighters and Jail Officers to be able to communicate with non-English speaking people is immense. So many times and in many situations, there is no time to find someone to assist in Spanish translation. Therefore, the need to have a good "working knowledge" of the

Spanish language is paramount. Wherever you may live or work, you will encounter a Spanish-speaking person. Spanish in the United States of America is the largest foreign spoken language. There are more Spanish speakers in the world than English speakers.

This book will instruct, guide and train anyone who has never studied the Spanish language and will better assist people who already have a basic knowledge of Spanish. The author hopes this will help everyone in their day-to-day jobs. This book is written as a self-teaching guide. With this in mind, the author has presented the teaching of essentials of the Spanish language at a beginning level and in a practical and pleasant manner.

Features Contained Within this Book

- Pronunciations of the Spanish alphabet, vowels, and how to break down ***any*** word in Spanish and pronounce the word with a high degree of proficiency.

- Understanding basic Spanish grammar, presented in an easy and concise manner of instruction.

- Vocabulary of words used specifically in law enforcement, unique to situations encountered in fieldwork and drug investigations.

- A thorough explanation of how Spanish verbs work, and shortcuts to conjugations.

- Words and phrases demonstrated through the use of phonics to help the reader pronounce Spanish words.

- Cultural explanations of the *Hispanic* household to include the hierarchy of the family unit and celebrations specific to the Hispanic culture.

This book offers a fundamental and alternative way to the instructional methodology of most Spanish language text books available today. With all of this being said, let's get started………………….. *¡Vamanos!*

TABLE OF CONTENTS

I. BASIC GRAMMAR

Communicating and
Understanding Spanish……………………………………….11
The Spanish Alphabet …………………………………..12
The Spanish Vowels………………………………………14
Word Structure……………………………………………15
Phrase Structure…………………………………………..15
Grammar…………………………………………………..11
Sentence Structure………………………………………..25
Definite and Indefinite Articles…………………………..25
Pronouns…………………………………………………..33
Demonstrative Pronouns………………………………….33
Verbs – Types, Use and Conjugation…..………………..36
Adjectives…………………………………………………31
Gender – Masculine and Feminine………………………17
Nouns - Singular and Plural………………………………17
Prepositions – Uses of "FOR"……………………………27
Cognates…………………………………………………..68

II. GENERAL KNOWLEDGE

The Human Body…………………………………..............76
The Colors…………………………………………………74
Telling Time – Hours, Days, Weeks, Months……………..80
The Numbers – Cardinal and Ordinal…………………….70
Buildings – Home/Business and Contents………………..146
Clothing Description……………………………………..90
Directions (Compass)……………………………………..88

Measurements..88
Vehicle Descriptions....................................116
Food and Restaurant Terminology................224

III. THE HISPANIC FAMILY AND CULTURAL HIGHLIGHTS

Poverty and basic rights of Mexicans.............155
What is the definition of the term "Hispanic"?......154
Family Structure – Names and Last Names.........160
The Traditional Family and its Hierarchy..........165
The Influence of religion within the culture.......159
Perception of Law Enforcement in the United States.........172

IV. APPLIED LESSONS

Alcohol and Open Containers........................110
Assault and Robbery Investigations...............183
Booking Terminology..................................204
Commands...103, 216
Commercial Vehicle Inspections....................120
Danger Expressions....................................129
Directions..88
Domestic Violence Investigations..................181
Drug Investigations....................................143
DWI/DUI Investigations..............................108
Felony Car Stop...103
Human Trafficking.....................................228
Injury Questions / Phraseology....................117
Metric Measurements..................................89
Miranda Warning......................................179
Missing or Lost Child..................................200
Sex Crimes..186
Suspect Descriptions..................................184
Traffic Emergencies....................................95

Types of Vehicles..116
Vehicle Traffic Stop...95
Weapon Terminology...129

CHAPTER ONE

ASPECTS OF SPANISH GRAMMAR

COMMUNICATING AND UNDERSTANDING SPANISH

To communicate with another person is to transmit a thought or an idea, something we want another one to know. The organization of thoughts and ideas originate the messages we send to others. This allows us to transmit precise and clear information if we use the correct words. When we wish others to receive some explanation of rules and regulations, these messages must be short and easy to understand, regardless of the language.

The clue to good communication resides in the fact that it must be understood by the receiver. A law enforcement officer may issue an order, explain a rule, or help a neighbor, but if he/she does not use the correct terminology, they ***will not*** be understood. As difficult as it is to communicate our thoughts in the same language, imagine how much harder it is to cross the language barrier. Furthermore, when it comes to the Law Enforcement profession, it is absolutely necessary that the message be thoroughly understood by the giver as well as by the receiver.

In exercising good communication, for proper understanding, we must try to understand and the language of the receiver. This is especially important in the day-to-day exercise of the duties of Law Enforcement officers.

Communication: The exchange of information between people, e.g. by means of speaking, writing, or using a common system of signs or behavior.

Understanding: The ability to perceive and explain the meaning or the nature of somebody or something.

No amount of talking, yelling, writing or hand waving will convey our message. The only measure of success is the clarity, brevity, and precision of our communication. This type of communication requires little explanation and avoids dangerous discussions. In a life and death situation, it is of the utmost importance to use the correct communication. The sphere of crime and delinquency is spread all over the world, and the possibility of encountering immigrants from many different cultural backgrounds is an everyday occurrence. Therefore, Law Enforcement officers must prepare themselves to understand and communicate their questions, orders, and directives in the most appropriate manner.

To this end, this book will provide simple, concise, short phrases and sentences in Spanish that may be used by Law Enforcement officers as they conduct their duties.

THE ALPHABET

In the Spanish language, grammar rules are basically the same as in English. Of course, there is always the consideration of understanding grammar; grammar is what makes any language work. Bearing this in mind, let's begin with the Spanish alphabet. Please remember, as in the English alphabet, each individual letter of the alphabet has a unique sound for each letter. The same applies to the Spanish Alphabet, each letter takes on a unique sound. Once you take the letters and place them into a word, the word takes on the sound of the word - the same in both languages.

Letter	**Name**	**Example**
A	*a* (as in palm)	Ana
B	*be* (as in bay)	Bueno
C	*ce* (as in say)	Celia
CH*	*che* (as CH)	as in Chain

D	*de* (as in day)	David
E	*e* (as in ay)	Elena (like a long "ay")
F	*efe* (as in efay)	Francisco
G	*ge* (as in hay)	Gerardo
H	*hache* (as in achay)	Hernández **("H" is always silent)**
I	*i* (as in ee)	Ignacio
J	*jota* (as in hoetah)	Juan **("J" sounds like "H" as in English)**
K	*ka* (as in kah)	Kilo
L	*ele* (as in ehlay)	Latino
LL*	*elle* (as in eyeh)	Llave **("LL" sounds like "Y" in English)**
M	*eme* (as in ehmay)	Martínez
N	*ene* (as in ehnay)	Nora
Ñ	*eñe* (as in ehnyay)	Cañón (like "ny" in canyon)
O	*o* (as in oh)	Oso (like "o" in obey)
P	*pe* (as in pay)	Pedro
Q	*qu* (as in coo)	Quintana
R	*ere* (as in ehray)	Mario
RR	*erre* (as in ehrray)	Roberto
S	*ese* (as in ehsay)	Sara
T	*te* (as in tay)	Tomás
U	*u* (as in oooh)	(like "oo" in moon)
V	*ve* (vey)	Victoria
W	*doble ve* (dohblay vey)	Wilson (same sound as in English)
X	*equis* (as in aykees)	Xerox (like in English)
Y	*i griega* (as in ee)	Yo (like "you")
Z	*seta* (as in saytah)	Zapato **(like a soft "s")**

*The letters **CH** and **LL** have been officially removed from the Spanish Alphabet. Even though they have been removed, throughout the course of this book, they have been included as there will be many words that still contain the **CH** and the **LL**.*

INTRODUCTION TO THE SPANISH SOUND SYSTEM

The alphabet and the Spanish sound system are the basic keys to learning the language. In Spanish, each letter has one, **and only one,** sound, with the exception of "**c**" and "**g**". The letters **c** and **g** can either have a hard sound or a soft sound at the beginning of the word, respectively. Therefore, you <u>*CAN*</u> read and pronounce Spanish correctly and easily remember these basic rules.

The consonants in Spanish do not differ significantly from those in English.

The vowels in Spanish – **a, e, i, o, u** have the following sounds:

a	*a (ah)*	Like "a" in father
e	*e (ay)*	Like the long "a" in English
i	*i (ee)*	Like "ee" as in see
o	*o (oh)*	Like "o" as in boat
u	*u (ooh)*	Like "oo" as in moon

Unlike English grammar, the sounds of the vowels in Spanish remain the same. By this, there are no long or short vowels. For the purpose of this book, let's say, every vowel in every word is pronounced and the vowel sound remains the same. Of course, as in English, there are a few grammatical rules in the Spanish language where certain vowels become silent; again, for the beginning learner, just pronounce every vowel. As you become more experienced in the Spanish language, you will begin to seen the nuances pertaining to the vowel rules.

★ *I cannot stress enough of the following:*

The ***VOWELS*** are the **_secret to pronouncing_** words in Spanish! Once you know the Spanish vowels, you can, and I stress, you can absolutely pronounce every word in Spanish either correctly or very close to the correct pronunciation! Please, practice, practice, and practice your vowels!

SPANISH PHONETICS THEORY

In the Spanish language, grammar rules are basically the same as in English. The nice thing about Spanish is that almost every word can be broken down to its simplest form and **you can** pronounce the word. Along with the phonetic breakdown comes the understanding of syllabication. **Syllabication** merely means that you break the word to syllables, and remembering how the vowels sound *(the sound of the vowels remains constant),* you can easily say the word. If there is an accent mark present, it will denote the most emphatic (or stressed) syllable in the word. *Spanish is truly a phonetic language, how it sounds is how it is spelled and pronounced.*

Please remember, the "Ñ" is a unique letter of the Spanish alphabet. The mark above the letter Ñ is called a **Tilde**. This is different from a vowel that has an **accent mark** above the vowel.

Only vowels will have an accent mark above the vowel, never a consonant!

Example: **Gramática es fácil.** (*Grah-mah-teeh-kah ays fah-seel*) - Grammar is easy.

Break down the words into syllables: Gra/ má/ ti/ ca es fá/ cil.

Phonetically: (*Grah* – **mah** – *teeh* – *kah* – *ehs* – **fah** – *seel*)

Example:

¿Cuántos años tiene? (***kwan**-tohs ah-nyohs tee-eh-neh*) - How old are you?

Break down into syllables: Cuán/ tos a/ños tie/ne?

Phonetically: **(kwan** – *tohs* – *ah* – *nyohs* – *tee* – *eh* – *neh)*

REMEMBER:

The Spanish vowels remain constant!!! Unlike vowels in English grammar, with long, short and silent sounds, Spanish vowels stay the same with very, very few grammatical exceptions. Practice your vowels. Once you hear them in your mind's ear, **you can** pronounce any word in Spanish! The more you practice word syllabication and phonetics, the easier it will become for you to read and speak Spanish. Furthermore, when learning a foreign language, learn one phrase at a time, as opposed to an individual word at a time. By this process of remembering phrases, you can begin to put them together to make sentences. You can also cut and paste one phrase to another and create an entirely new phrase. Before you know it, your phrases will become sentences and they will lead to paragraphs and full conversations.

THE WRITTEN ACCENT

Spanish words carry **one, and only one** phonetic stress. This stress is marked with a tilde or written accent mark (') according to some grammar rules. There are three rules that we need to remember:

1. Words that are stressed on the *last syllable* need an accent if the last letter is an *n*, an *s, or a vowel.* Also, the word must have two or more syllables. Examples: *está, estás, están, aquí, jardín, canción, caminé, inglés, camión*

2. Words that are stressed on the ***next-to-the-last syllable*** need an accent if the last letter is any consonant except "***n***" or "***s.***" Examples:

cáncer, cárcel, cóndor, fácil, lápiz

3. Words that are stressed ***two syllables before the last*** <u>always</u> need an accent. With these types of words, the last letter has nothing to do with the accent. Examples:

águila, árabe, cámara, décimo, mínimo, número, pájaros, público, víctima,

4. To separate a diphthong (two vowels together) in the following combinations: "***io***", "***ia***" or "***ua***", you place an accent over the first vowel. Examples:

capitanía, corrían, día, fotografía, grúa, mío, policía, tíos

NOUNS

GENDER OF NOUNS

A ***<u>noun</u>*** is a word used to denote a person, place, thing, or idea. Example:

Person: John, girl, dentist
Place: garden, university, Colombia
Thing: book, car, tomato
Idea: liberty, despair, intelligence

In Spanish, all nouns and adjectives have Gender, either masculine or feminine; ("**el**" and "**la**" both mean "the.") Examples:

El chico (masculine) - The boy
La chica (feminine) - The girl

El jardín (masculine) - The garden

La universidad (feminine) - The university

El libro (masculine) - The book

La revista (feminine) - The magazine

El miedo (masculine) - The fear

La libertad (feminine) - The liberty

Why do you care whether a noun or adjective is masculine or feminine? Good question! As you shall see in upcoming lessons, Spanish places a great deal more emphasis on gender than does English. The idea that nouns have gender seems perfectly natural when the noun stands for a living creature. This is because in English, living creatures often have different names, depending upon whether they are male or female.
Example:

Man - woman

Tiger - tigress

Actor - actress

The following Spanish **nouns** all denote living creatures:

El **gato** (the male cat)   La **gata** (the female cat)
El **perro** (the male dog)   La **perra** (the female dog)
El **chico** (the boy)   La **chica** (the girl)
El **abuelo** (the grandfather)   La **abuela** (the grandmother)

How are all of these masculine nouns alike? What do you notice about the last letter of these nouns?

El **gato** (*ehl gah-toh*)
El **perro** (*ehl peh-rroh*)
El **chico** (*ehl che-koh*)
El **abuelo** (*ehl ah-bu-eh-loh*)

How are all of these feminine nouns alike? What do you notice about the last letter of these nouns?

La **gata** (*lah gah-tah*)
La **perra** (*lah peh-rrah*)
La **chica** (*lah che-kah*)
La **abuela** (*lah ah-bu-eh-lah*)

Nouns that end in "o" are **usually** masculine; nouns that end in "a" are **usually** feminine. Notice the word *usually*. There are exceptions to these two rules and you will soon learn them.

One cannot predict the gender of a noun, except in the case of living creatures. One cannot predict the gender of a noun that stands for a non-living thing. Don't try to analyze the nature of the object, looking for some inherent masculine or feminine quality; it won't work! Take a guess. Do you think the Spanish word for "dress" is masculine or feminine? You might expect it to be feminine, since a dress is an article of clothing worn by females. Actually, the word for "dress" is a masculine word: el vestido *(ehl vehs-tee-doh).*

Take another guess. Do you think the Spanish word for "necktie" is masculine or feminine? You might expect it to be masculine, since a necktie is an article of clothing worn by men. Actually, the word for "necktie" is a feminine word: la corbata *(lah korh-bah-tah).*

When you learn a new noun, you should also learn its corresponding (masculine or feminine) definite article (el, los or la, las). There are several reasons for this:

- Because you cannot predict the gender of most nouns.
- Because not every noun that ends in "o" is masculine, and not every noun that ends in "a" is feminine.
- Because many nouns end in letters other than "o" or "a."
- Because the definite article (el, la) is your clue as to whether a noun is masculine or feminine. Masculine nouns that end in a consonant often have a corresponding feminine form that ends in "**a**."

El profesor *(ehl proh-fehs-soohr)*
La profesora *(lah proh-fehs-soh-rah)*
El doctor *(ehl dohk-tohr)*
La doctora *(lah dohk-toh-rah)*
El señor *(ehl seh-nyohr)*
La señora *(lah seh-noyh-rah)*

Some nouns that refer to people use the same form for both masculine and feminine. These nouns indicate their gender by the corresponding article (*el* or *la*).

El estudiante *(ehl es-stoo-dee-ahn-teh)*
La estudiante *(lah es-stoo-dee-ahn-teh)*
El pianista *(ehl peh-ah-nees-stah)*
La pianista *(lah peh-an-nees-stah)*
El artista *(ehl ahr-tee-stah)*
La artista *(lah ahr-tee-stah)*

Nouns that end in *-sión*, "*ción*," "*dad*," "*tad*," "*tud*," "*umbre*," are feminine.

La televisión *(lah teh-leh-vee-see-ohn)* - the television
La decisión *(lah deh-cee-see-ohn)* - the deci*sion*
La conversación *(lah kohn verh-sah-see-ohn)* - the conversation
La habitación *(lah ha-beeh-tah-see-ohn)* - the room
La ciudad *(lah see-oo-dahd)* - the city
La universidad *(lah oo-nee-vehr-see-dahd)* - the university
La dificultad *(lah dee-fee-kuhl-tahd)* - the difficulty
La libertad *(lah lee-berh-tahd)* - the liberty

La actitud *(lah ahk-tee-tood)* - the attitude
La gratitud *(lah grah-tee-tood)* - the gratitude

Some nouns that end in "a" are masculine.

El agua *(ehl ah-wah)* - the water
El día *(ehl dee-ah)* - the day
El mapa *(ehl mah-pah)* - the map
El sofá *(ehl soh-fah)* - the sofa
El arma de fuego *(ehl ahr-mah de foo-eh-goh)* - the firearm
El problema *(ehl proh-bleh-mah)* - the problem
El telegrama *(ehl teh-leh-grah-mah)* - the telegram
El programa *(ehl proh-grah-mah)* - the program
El sistema *(ehl sees-teh-m*ah) - the system
El poema *(ehl po-eh-mah)* - the poem
El tema *(ehl teh-mah)* - the theme
El clima *(ehl kle-mah)* - the climate
El idioma *(ehl ee-dee-oh-mah)* - the language
El planeta *(ehl plah-neh-tah)* - the planet

A few nouns that end in "o" are actually feminine, and should be memorized:

La mano *(lah mah-noh)* - the hand
La radio *(lah rah-dee-oh)* - the radio

Some of the basics of nouns and their gender:

(1) Many nouns that denote living things have both a masculine and feminine form.
(2) **Most nouns/adjectives that end in "o" are masculine.**
(3) **Most nouns/adjectives that end in "a" are feminine.**
(4) Masculine nouns that end in consonant often have a corresponding feminine form that ends in "a."
(5) Some nouns that refer to people use the same word for masculine and feminine. Their gender is indicated by the corresponding article (*el* or *la*).

(6) Nouns that end in "sion," "ción," "dad," "tad," "tud," "umbre," are feminine.
(7) Many nouns that end in "a" are masculine.
(8) A few nouns that end in "o" are feminine.

These are the basic rules for determining the gender of a noun. There are a few more things to learn, and they will be covered later. Remember, it is best when learning a new noun, to learn it complete with its definite article (**el, los or la, las**).

PLURAL FORM OF NOUNS

If a noun ends in a *vowel*, simply add an "s" to make it plural.

Libro - libros   (*lee-broh, lee-brohs*)   (book – books)

Pluma – plumas   (*pluh-mah, pluh-mahs*)   (pen – pens)

Chico – chicos   (*chee-koh, chee-kohs*)   (boy – boys)

Señora – señoras   (*seh-noy-rah, seh-noyh-rahs*) (lady – ladies)

If a noun ends in a *consonant*, add "es" to make the plural. Examples:

Profesor - profesores   (*proh-feh-sohr, proh-feh-soh-res*) (teacher – teachers)

Ciudad – ciudades   (*see-ooh-dahd, see-ooh-dahd-es*)   (city – cities)

Canción – canciones   (*cahn-see-ohn, cahn-see-ohn-es*) (song – songs)

Metal – metales   (*meh-tahl, meh-tahl-es*)   (metal – metals)

The definite article (el, la) also changes to the plural form. "El" becomes "los" and "la" becomes "las."

Examples:

    El libro – **los** libros
    La pluma – **las** plumas
    El chico – **los** chicos
    La señora – **las** señoras

If a noun ends in "**ión**" add "**es**" and drop the written accent.

Examples:

    El avión – los aviones (*lohs ah-vee-ohn-es*) (the airplane – the airplanes)

    La sección – las secciones (*lahs sehk-see-ohn-es*) (the section – the sections)

    La nación – las naciones (*lahs nah-see-ohn-es*) (the nation – the nations)

If a noun ends in "**z**" change the "z" to "**c**" and add "**es**." Examples:

    El lápiz – los lápices (*lohs lah-pee-sehs*) (the pencil – the pencils)

    La voz – las voces (*lahs voh-cehs*) (the voice – the voices)

    La actriz – las actrices
(*lahs ahk-tree-sehs*) (the actress – the actresses)

When the plural refers to two or more nouns of different gender, the **masculine** form is used.

Examples:

Dos gatos + seis gatas = Ocho gatos (masculine)
Un perro + ocho perras = Nueve perros (masculine)

A few nouns are "compound" nouns; this means that they are formed by combining two words into one; for instance: abre + latas = abrelatas (can opener). These nouns always have a masculine gender, and the plural is denoted by the corresponding article. Examples:

El abrelatas – los abrelatas (*lohs ah-breh-lah-tahs*) (the can openers)
El paraguas – los paraguas (*lohs pah-rah-goo-ahs*) (the umbrellas)
Un sobrecama – Unos sobrecamas (*oo-nohs soh-breh-cah-mahs*) some bed covers, quilts)

To review, the rules for making nouns and adjectives plural:

(1) If a noun/adjective ends in a vowel, simply add "s."
(2) If a noun/adjective ends in a consonant, simply add "es."
(3) If a noun ends in a "z," change the "z" to "c" befores adding "es."
(4) If a noun ends in "ión," drop the written accent before adding "es."
(5) If the plural refers to a mixed (gender) group, always use the masculine gender.
(6) For compound (masculine) nouns, use the article in its plural form (los, unos).

DEFINITE ARTICLES

Now that we have examined the gender make-up of nouns in the Spanish language, let's look at the **definite articles**. By far, these are easier to remember. The definite article indicates a specific noun. There are four definite articles in Spanish, and they correspond to the word "**the**" in English. They are **el** and **la**, and their plural counterparts, **los** and **las**.

Gender	Singular	Plural
Masculine Masculino	**El** El libro El hombre El rifle	**Los** Los libros Los hombres Los rifles
Feminine Femenino	**La** La mesa La mujer La pistola	**Las** Las mesas Las mujeres Las pistolas

EX: **¿Dónde está *el* libro?** (*dohn-deh es-stah ehl lee-broh*)
(Where is the book?)

EX: ***Las* chicas no quieren comer *los* tacos** (*lahs chee-kahs noh ke-eer-ehn ko-mehr lohs tah-kohs*) The girls do not want to eat the tacos.

The definite article is also used in Spanish to indicate the general sense of a noun. In English, and article is not used in this situation.

EX: **Me gusta *el* café** (*meh goos-stah ehl ka-feh*) I like coffee.
EX: **¡Así es *la* vida!** (*ah-see ees lah vee-dah*) That's life!

INDEFINITE ARTICLES

The **indefinite** article usually refers to an unspecified person or thing. The Spanish indefinite article is sometimes confusing to beginning Spanish speakers, because it must agree in *gender and number* with the noun it modifies, and it doesn't always correspond to an article in other languages. It may be helpful to remember that in Spanish, if you have a noun, you will almost always have an article (definite or indefinite) as well. There are four indefinite articles in English: **a, an, some and any** (a book, an apple, some trees, any magazines). In Spanish, there are four indefinite articles: "**un**" and "**una**," (singular) with their plural counterparts, "**unos**" and "**unas**."

Gender	Singular	Plural
Masculine Masculino	**Un** Un libro Un hombre Un rifle	**Unos** Unos libros Unos hombres Unos rifles
Feminine Femenino	**Una** Una mesa Una mujer Una pistola	**Unas** Unas mesas Unas mujeres Unas pistolas

EX: **Quiero *un* libro** (*kee-yero oon lee-broh*) (I want a book)
    Tengo *una* idea (*tehn-goh oo-nah ee-deh-ah*) I have an idea.

The **indefinite** article can also refer to just "one" of something.

EX: **Hay *un* estudiante en la sala.** *(eye oon ehs-too-dee-ahn-teh ehn lah sah-lah)* There is one student in the room.

The **plural indefinite** article means "some."

EX: **Compro *unas* plumas**. *(kohm-proh oo-nahs ploo-mahs)* I buy some pens.

When referring to a person's profession, the indefinite article is not used in Spanish, although it is used in English.

EX: **Soy policía**. *(soh-ee poh-lee-see-ah)* I am a police officer.

PREPOSITIONS

The main prepositions in Spanish are: "a, ante, bajo, con, contra, de, desde, en, entre, hacia, hasta, para, por, según, sin, sobre and tras." You don't have to remember all of them. However, it is important to learn the difference between "**para**" and "**por**," since both of these translate from the same English word: "**for**."

Thanks *for* the information   **Gracias *por* la información.**
(*Grah-see-ahs pohr lah een-fohr-mah-see-ohn*)

This car is *for* Steven   **Este carro es *para* Esteban.**
(*ess-teh kah-rroh ehs pah-rah Es-teh-bahn*)

To learn to use "**por**" and "**para**" correctly, you need to do two things:

(1) Learn the rules for using "por" and "para."
(2) Memorize the example sentences.

(1) **"Por"** has many uses, so it is the more problematic of the two.

   Rule: To express gratitude or apology.

   Example: **Gracias por la ayuda.**   (Thanks for the help)
   Rule: For multiplication and division.

Example: **Tres por tres son nueve.** (Three times three equals nine.)

Rule: For velocity, frequency and proportion
Example: **Voy a la playa dos veces por semana.** (I go to the beach twice per week)

Rule: Meaning "through," "along," "by" or "in the area of"
Example: **¿No quieres caminar por el parque?** (Don't you want to walk through the park?)

Rule: when talking about exchange, including sales.

Example: **Ella me dio cien dólares por el carro.** (She gave me one hundred dollars for the car)

Rule: To express a length of time.

Example: **Yo estudié por cuatro horas.** (I studied for four hours.)

Rule: To indicate means of communication or transportation.

Example: **Prefiero viajar por avion y hablar por teléfono cellular.** (I prefer to travel by airplane and speak by cellular phone)

Rule: "Estar por" means to be ready to, or inclined to do something.

Example: **El taxi está por salir sin nosotros.** (The taxi is about to leave without us)

Example: **Estoy por irme muy lejos.** (I'm in the mood for going far away.)

(2) "**Para**", in contrast, has relatively fewer uses.

Rule: To indicate destination

Example: El hombre salió para Cancún. (The man left for Cancún)

Rule: To show the use or purpose of a thing
Example: La vida es para vivirla. (Life is for living)

Rule: To mean "in order to" or "for the purpose of"

Example: Para hacer una torta, mezcle los ingredientes. (To make a cake, mix the ingredients)

Rule: To indicate a recipient

Example: Este regalo es para Usted. (This gift is for you)

Rule: To express a deadline or specific time.

Example: Necesito los pantalones para el Viernes. (I need the pants by Friday)

Rule: To express a contrast from what is expected.

Example: Para una niña, habla muy bien. (For a child, she speaks very well)

"**Por**" and "**para**" can also be used to ask questions. "¿Por qué?" means "Why? (for what reason)," while "¿Para qué?" means "What for? (for what purpose)."

¿Por qué estudia español? (*Pohr keh ees-toh-dee-ah eh-spah-nyohl?*) (Why do you study Spanish?)

Porque es un necesario para mi trabajo. (*Pohr-keh ehs neh-seh-sah-ree-oh pah-rah mee trah-bah-ho*) (Because it's necessary for my job)

¿Para qué estudia español? (*Pah-rah keh ehs-stuh-dee-ah ehs-pah-nyohl?*) (For what purpose do you study Spanish?)

Para poder hablar español profesionalmente. (*Pah-rah poh-dehr-hah-blahr ehs-pah-nyohl pro-fehs-see-oh-nahl-mehn-teh*) (In order to speak Spanish professionally)

List of Spanish Prepositions	
a (to, at)	en vez de (instead of)
al (upon)	en (in, on)
al lado de (beside)	encima de (above, on top)
ante (before)	enfrente de (in front of)
antes de (before)	entre (between, among)
bajo (under)	fuera de (outside)
cerca de (near)	hacia (towards)
como (like)	hasta (until)
con (with)	lejos de (far from)
contra (against)	menos (except)
de (from, of, about)	para (for, in order to)
debajo de (under, beneath)	por (for, on account of)
delante de (in front of)	salvo (except)
dentro de (inside)	según (according to)
desde (since)	sin (without)
después de (after)	sobre (about, above/on)
detrás de (behind)	tras (after)

ADJECTIVES

Adjectives are descriptive words used to point to a certain quality of a noun, or to distinguish a particular noun from a group of similar objects. Contrary to English grammar rules, **_the adjective in Spanish follows the noun!_** For example, an adjective might describe the color of an object:

    The blue pen   **La pluma azul** (*lah ploo-mah ah-sool*)
    The brown pen   **La pluma café** (*lah ploo-mah kah-feh*)

In Spanish, most adjectives also have gender (masculine, feminine) which always match the gender of the noun. Example:

    The tall boy   **El chico alto** (*ehl chee-koh ahl-toh*)
    The tall girl   **La chica alta** (*lah chee-kah ahl-tah*)

In addition, adjectives are also used in the singular and the plural, and these forms always match the accompanying noun. Example:

    The tall boys   **Los chicos altos** (*lohs chee-kohs ahl-tos*)
    The tall girls   **Las chicas altas** (*lahs chee-kahs ahl-tas*)

The correct form of the adjective depends upon the noun it modifies. Is the noun masculine or feminine, singular or plural? The ending of the noun and its qualifying adjective must be the same. Example:

    Red book   **Libr<u>o</u> roj<u>o</u>** (*lee-broh roh-hoh*)
    Red pen   **Plum<u>a</u> roj<u>a</u>** (*ploo-mah roh-hah*)
    Black cats   **Gat<u>os</u> negr<u>os</u>** (*gah-tohs neh-grohs*)
    White cows   **Vac<u>as</u> blanc<u>as</u>** (*vah-kahs blahn-kahs*)

Most adjectives end in "**o**" (masculine) or "**a**" (feminine). Adjectives that end in "**e**" or in "**a consonant**," do not have gender; in other words, the same form applies to both masculine and feminine.

However, all adjectives must be expressed in "**singular**" or "**plural**." Examples:

The smart boy	**El chico inteligente** (*ehl chee-koh een-teh-lee-hen-teh*)
The smart girl	**La chica inteligente** (*lah chee-kah een-teh-lee-hen-teh*)
The popular boys	**Los chicos populares** (*lohs chee-kohs poh-puh-lah-rehs*)
The popular girls	**Las chicas populares** (*lahs chee-kahs poh-puh-lah-rehs*)

REVIEW:

(1) Adjectives that end in "**o**" (masculine) change to "**a**" (feminine).
(2) Adjectives that end in "**e**" or "**a consonant**" do not change to the feminine form.
(3) **All** adjectives must be in the "**singular**" or "**plural**" form, depending on the noun they modify.

POSSESSIVE ADJECTIVES

Unstressed forms of possessive adjectives stand before the noun they modify, agreeing in number with the thing possessed, not with the possessor, an example: **su lápiz** - his pencil, her pencil, your pencil, their pencil; **sus libros** - his books, her books, your books or their books.

	Singular	Plural
1st person	**mi, mis** – my	**nuestro(s), nuestra (s)** – our
2nd person (formal)	**su, sus** – your	**su, sus** – yours
3rd person	**su, sus** – his, hers, its	**su, sus** – theirs

Stressed forms of possessive adjectives follow the noun they modify and are used primarily in direct address, in exclamations, and as equivalents of English *of mine, of his, of hers, of theirs* and so on. An example is: **Buenos días, amigo mío,** *Good morning, my friend.*

        Singular (*masc.fem.*)   Plural *masc.fem*)

	Singular (*masc.fem.*)	Plural (*masc.fem*)
1st person	**mío(s), mía(s)** my	**nuestro(s), nuestra(s)**
2nd person	**suyo(s), suya (s)** your	
3rd person	**suyo(s), suya(s)** his, hers, its	**suyo(s), suya(s)**

DEMONSTRATIVE PRONOUNS
NUMBER AND GENDER

The demonstrative pronoun must agree in gender and in number with the noun for which they stand., example: **éste libro**, *this book.* Whereas **éstas plumas**, *these pens*, is plural and agree in number and gender. Another example is: **Aquél hombre**, *that man* (over there), or **aquéllas mujeres**, *those women* (over there).

	Singular	Plural
Masculine	**éste** this, this one (near me)	**éstos** these (near me)
Feminine	**ésta** this, this one (near me)	**éstas** these (near me)
Masculine	**ése** that, that one (near you)	**ésos** those (near you)
Feminine	**ésa** that, that one (near you)	**ésas** those (near you)
Masculine	**aquél** that, that one (yonder)	**aquéllos** those (yonder)
Feminine	**aquélla** that, that one (yonder)	**aquéllas** those (yonder)

PERSONAL PRONOUNS
(SUBJECT PRONOUNS)

In Spanish, as in English, a verb is an action word. The verb must be conjugated to relate directly to the person (s) or thing (s) that indicates the action. In order to do this, you must add a "pronoun" to the verb to show who is performing the action. For example: I speak, you walk, she sings, we dance, you read and they eat. The words "I, you, he, she, it, we, you all and they" are called Subject Pronouns. This means they are used to conjugate verbs. Spanish has corresponding subject pronouns. In Spanish, some of these pronouns also have gender (masculine, feminine). Here's a list of the English subject pronouns and their Spanish equivalents:

I	**Yo** (*yoh*)
You	**Tú** (informal) (*too*), **Usted** (formal) (*oo-stehd*)
He, she	**Él, Ella** (*ehl, eh-yah*)
We	**Nosotros, Nosotras** (*noh-soh-trohs, noh-soh-trahs*)
You all (everyone)	**Ustedes** (*oo-steh-dehs*)
They/Those (males/females)	**Ellos, Ellas** (*eh-yohs, eh-yahs*)

Although in English the same word is used for both the singular and the plural "you," in Spanish these two pronouns are different. Each of the following is correct:

> You have a head light out, sir.
> You (plural suspects) have committed a crime.

In the first sentence, "you" refers to the singular (*sir*); in the second sentence, "you" refers to the plural (*suspects*). As stated above, there are two ways the English word "you" can be expressed in Spanish:

> **Tú** (informal), **usted** (formal)   This is the singular form
> **Ustedes**   This is the plural form

Usted is more formal and is generally used to express respect. *Tú* is more familiar and is used among friends, coworkers, relatives, or when addressing a child.

Speaking to a suspect:	**usted**
Speaking to your spouse:	**tú**
Speaking to your supervisor:	**usted**
Speaking to your friend:	**tú**

Spanish is gender-specific contrary to English. This is very evident in the subject pronouns. Examine the word "nosotros." This means "we" in the sense of a group containing at least one male. If the group contains only females, the word "nosotras" is used. So, in Spanish, there are two ways to say "we:"

Nosotros	we (solely masculine or mixed group of males and females)
Nosotras	we (feminine, all females and no males, not even a small male child)

The same idea applies to the English word "they":

Ellos	they (masculine or mixed group)
Ellas	they (feminine, all females)

Author's Note

*Through the course of this instructional book, I will use the subject pronoun "**Usted**" in lieu of the "**Tú**." I have a couple of thoughts as to why I have chosen this. First and foremost, in law enforcement, you must **always** exhibit professional decorum! Thusly, by addressing everyone who you come in contact with, you cannot go wrong in using the "Usted" form. Remember, Tú is familiar and does not demonstrate professionalism. Secondly, it is **one** less verb conjugation to remember, this will become self-evident very soon when we begin to conjugate verbs in Spanish.*

VERBS

Through the years of experience teaching Spanish language I have found verbs as one of the most difficult aspects when learning the language. In every course taught, I ask the students what the one Spanish language grammar issue is giving them the greatest challenge; the overwhelming response is ***verb conjugation***. Understanding this problem with beginners in the Spanish language, I have incorporated a system of verb conjugation, which makes conjugations easy to understand. The more you practice verb conjugations, the faster you will be able to formulate your sentences and carry on a conversation.

In the Spanish language, there are regular and irregular verbs. By this, regular verbs follow the same pattern of conjugation, and irregular verbs change somehow within their conjugations. Henceforth, let's tackle the ***regular*** verbs first. The Spanish language stresses singular and plural, not only in verbs, but also in all aspects of the language.

You can purchase dozens of Spanish language books trying to understand how to conjugate the verbs. Bearing this in mind, I have formatted a simple way to break down verbs into a simple to use format that will make learning Spanish verbs much easier. Earlier in this book I listed Subject Pronouns. **The below graph is created to facilitate how to match up the pronouns to the verb conjugation.**

SINGULAR	PLURAL
I – **Yo**	**Nosotros / Nosotras** - We
You –**Usted** He – **Él** She – **Ella** (It - singular)	**Ustedes** ⎰ You All ⎱ Every One - Every Body **Ellos** The/All Males- Or Mixed Group **Ellas** The/All Females (It – plural)

Diagram #1

What is shown above will be identified as your "**Building Block**" to verb conjugation! Please study the diagram above. Please notice the following: The diagram is divided into two vertical columns - left (singular) and right (plural) pronouns. From this point forward, we will use this **Building Block** diagram in *ALL* verb conjugations.

In the upper left area, this area will *always* refer to: "**I**."

In the lower left area, this area will *always* refer to: "**You**," "**He**," "**She**," and "**It -singular**."

In the upper right area, this area will *always* refer to: "**We**."

In the lower right area, this area will *always* refer to: "**Everyone**," "**They (males)**," "**They (females)**," "**It-plural**."

When we begin to conjugate our verbs, you will simply lift this diagram and place it onto the corresponding verb diagram. By doing this, ALL of the four divided sections will line up and it will make understanding how and why the pronouns (and eventually nouns) line up. The above diagram will act as a "transparency" sheet covering the verbs that are conjugated. This will make even more sense in a few minutes. Put this to the side for now and let's look at the Spanish verbs.

Now let's talk about the makeup of what a verb is in Spanish. A verb in the Spanish language *always* means "**to**" plus the action. This is called the ***infinitive*** form of the verb, same as in the English language. Examples are: to walk (caminar), to talk (hablar), to run (correr), to fight (peliar), to drink (tomar) and so on. Almost all verbs consist of two parts in Spanish, those being the *stem* and the *ending*. In Spanish all verbs are categorized into three broad categories: 1. Verbs ending in **_AR_**; 2.Verbs ending in **_ER_** and 3. Verbs ending in **_IR_**.

Now let's look at what the meaning of **stem** and **ending** means. Let's look at the Spanish verb **hablar** – to speak. Once you begin to break down the Spanish verb, **habl** is the stem of the verb and **_ar_** is the ending. Let's look at another Spanish verb, "comer" to eat, **_com_** is the stem and **_er_** is the ending. Finally, let's look at vivir –to live, **_viv_** is the stem and **_ir_** is the ending.

Let's conjugate your first verb, "**Hablar**," (To Speak), in present indicative tense.

Remember, you save the stem, drop the "ar" ending and add the correct new ending to conjugate the verb. ***Simply put, once you remove the ending, write the stem in the four window areas of your building block, then add the correct ending to the verb.***

Yo (I), add the letter "**O**" = Yo **Hablo**, I speak.

Usted (You formal), Él (He), Ella (She), It, add the letter "**A**" = Usted, Él, Ella (it) **Habla**, you, he, she, it speaks.

Nosotros/as (We), add the letters "**AMOS**" = Nosotros/Nosotras **Hablamos**, we speak.

Ustedes (Everyone), *Ellos* (They Men), *Ellas* (They Women), add the letters "**AN**"= ***Hablan*** Ustedes, Ellas, Ellos, everyone, the males (or) mixed group, the females speak.

Below is the "***Building Block***" that is applied to the verb "**Hablar**."

SINGULAR   **PLURAL**

Yo Habl**o**	Nosotros/Nosotras Habl**amos**
Usted Él Habl**a** Ella It	Ustedes Ellos Habl**an** Ellas It (plural)

Diagram #2

Now, let's look at how the Building Block with the Subject Pronouns works with the conjugated verbs. Remember, the pronouns will act like a transparency and sit directly on top of the conjugated verb, no matter what verb you conjugate!

SINGULAR	PLURAL (Transparency)
I – **Yo**	We – **Nosotros/Nosotras**
You – **Usted**	You All Every One - **Ustedes** Everybody
He – **Él** She – **Ella**	The/All Males - **Ellos** Or Mixed Group The/All Females - **Ellas**
(It - singular)	(It – plural)

Diagram #3

Lay this transparency on top of the Verb Building Block and then you will have the correct pronouns lined up with the correct conjugated forms of the verb.

Yo Habl**o**	Nosotros/Nosotras Habl**amos**
Usted Él Habl**a** Ella It	Ustedes Ellos Habl**an** Ellas It (plural)

Diagram #4

If you look at the endings of He, She, (It), and You (formal), the ending is the same, likewise for, They (Men), They (Women), and They All. Since they share common endings, you will **_need to identify_** whom you are referring. So, you will need to say the subject pronoun along with the verb. If you do not, then there will be vagueness in how the verb is being used.

Examples: <u>You speak Spanish</u>. ***Usted habla Español.***

If you were just to say: "***Habla Español,***" it would not be clear who is speaking Spanish. It could be, *he speaks, she speaks, it speaks or you speak*, without the identifying pronoun or noun. Therefore, please use the pronoun (or noun) every time you conjugate a verb. As you get better in your skills, it will become easier and easier to use the pronoun along with the verb.

Author's Note

From this point forward, we will ALWAYS use the <u>*Pronoun Building Block to be placed "ON TOP OF" the conjugated verb NO MATTER WHAT THE VERB IS!*</u> *Please take the time to study the subject pronoun* <u>*Building Block*</u>*. In a short time, I will show you a way to easily study a sentence in English and be able to conjugate the verb and by a quick process of elimination, you can select the correct conjugated form of the verb, trust me on this! Also, I promised that I would explain what "IT" is, so here we go:*

In English as well as in Spanish we can replace a noun for a pronoun and vice versa. Several examples are as follows: "***The car is blue***". The word "**Car**" is the noun in this sentence. If you were speaking to someone and you and the other person knew that the subject of the conversation was the "**Car**", you could change the word from "**Car**" to the word "**It**." Then you could say, "**It** is blue."

Another example:

"Maria walks to the store." The word "*Maria*" is the noun. You could change the noun to a pronoun and state, "*She* walks to the store" and vice versa.

Another example:

"*Bob*" arrests the suspect. "*Bob*" is the noun in this sentence. You could also state the sentence (knowing you and the listener know it is Bob) and state, "*He*" arrests the suspect, or vice versa.

So, how will this help you in understanding how to conjugate your verbs? **Please read the following closely.**

In our verb **Building Block** window, there are *four* corners! The left vertical side is the "**Singular**" side and the right vertical side is the "**Plural**" side of the conjugated forms of each verb.

The top horizontal blocks (the "Yo" and the "Nosotros/as" blocks) will ALWAYS mean "YO" (I) top left and "NOSOTROS/AS (WE) top right. It can *never* mean anything other than these two definitions!!

The bottom two blocks will always have multiple meanings concerning which the action is referring to, i.e. You, He, She, It (singular) and You All, These/Those Males and These/Those Females.

So how can you figure out which conjugated form will be the correct form? Let's jump in –

Below, you will find some lines to translate. In the first example, "I speak," first look at the subject of the sentence. Is it singular or plural? It is singular. That example refers to only one person, "I." So, go to your conjugated window for the verb "Hablar," look at your four choices, find the window that refers to "I" and there is your correct choice. Now let's look at another example. In the sentence, "*Maria speaks*." In your *Pronoun Building Block* there is only pronouns displayed. So, how can you figure out which conjugated form will be the correct verb? Simply by a process of elimination. What is the subject of this sentence? Of course, **Maria** is. Is **Maria** singular or plural? Right, **Maria** is just one person, singular. Now go to your *Building Block* for the conjugated windows for the verb "Hablar." You can eliminate ½ of your four choices instantly. Since **Maria** is singular, **do not** look at the vertical *plural* forms. This only leaves the singular vertical column. Now you have two choices, top left or the bottom left. Since the top left is ALWAYS "YO" meaning "I," your only choice left is the bottom left window, "*Maria habla*."

So remember, always look at the subject of your sentence, is it singular or plural? By a process of elimination, you can quickly choose the correct conjugated verb.

One more example:

"*You and I speak*." What is the subject of this sentence? That's correct, **You** and **I** are the subjects of the sentence. Oh no, how will you go to your **Hablar** verb Building Block and use it to choose the correct conjugated verb? No problem, let's look at what we have in this example. Grammatically, **You** and **I** become a "*we*." In the example I offered, "**You and I speak**" could be re-written as being said, "**We** speak." But, that's not what was written. Knowing that "You and I" are considered a "we," go to the conjugated windows for "**Hablar**" and let's conduct a process of elimination. Since "You and I" are plural, eliminate the "*Singular*" vertical two choices. Now you have only two choices remaining, top right and bottom right vertical choices, the **Plural** side. Let's look at the bottom right – are we speaking about Everyone/You all? No. Are we speaking about Those/These males? No. Are we speaking about Those/These females? No. Therefore, the *ONLY* logical choice remaining in the top right choice, **Hablamos**. Your correct Spanish sentence will become, "*Usted y Yo hablamos*."

Translate the following into Spanish (word for word):

I speak				We speak				They (masc.) speak

Maria speaks			You (plural) speak		The baby speaks

You and I speak		The boy speaks			Gloria and I speak

Do you speak English?	He speaks English		They (fem.) speak

Now let's conjugate a regular verb that ends in "**er**," Comer in present indicative tense.

The pronouns are the same in the "**ER**" ending verbs as they are in "**AR**" ending verbs. Remember, drop the "**er**" ending, leaving "Com." Place the stem into the four Building Block windows and then add the correct endings. Notice that the endings change somewhat from the "AR" verbs. Notice this "ER" ending verb follows the same conjugating format. However, since it is an "ER" verb the endings differ from an "AR" verb. I eat ends in "**O**." He, she, (it), and you eat ends in "**E**." We eat ends in "**EMOS**," and they all, they (men) and they (women) ends in "**EN**."

Comer (To Eat)

SINGULAR	PLURAL
Yo Com**o**	Nosotros(as) Com**emos**
Usted Com**e** Él Com**e** Ella Com**e** (It) Com**e**	Ustedes Com**en** Ellos Com**en** Ellas Com**en** (It – plural) Com**en**

Diagram #5

Now, let's examine a verb that ends in "**IR**," **Vivir** (to live) in present indicative tense. The subject pronoun *Building Block* windows will again be the same. Remember, the pronouns will never change inside of the *Building Block*, only the verb conjugation will change. This is very important to remember! Notice this "**IR**" ending verb follows the same conjugating format. However, since it is an "**IR**" verb the endings differ from an "AR" and the "ER" verb. I live ends in "**O**." He, she, (it), and you live ends in "**E**." We live ends in "**IMOS**," and they all, they (men) and they (women) ends in "**EN**."

Vivir (To Live)

SINGULAR	PLURAL
Yo Viv**o**	Nosotros (as) Viv**imos**
Usted Viv**e** Él Viv**e** Ella Viv**e** (It) Viv**e**	Ustedes Viv**en** Ellos Viv**en** Ellas Viv**en** (It – Plural) Viv**en**

Diagram #6

Translate the following into Spanish (word for word):

I eat.   We eat.   They (fem.) eat.   Juan eats.

Juanita eats.   We live.   You (formal) live.   Pedro lives.

Author's Note

*I would highly encourage you to purchase a **Spanish-English / English-Spanish Dictionary** as well as a Spanish verb book, such as **501 Spanish Verbs** or something similar. There are many on the market, either in a brick and mortar building or on line. These two books will become your best sources to begin your road to Spanish language skills.*

The following is a short list of regular verbs that follow the same format as above. Take the time to practice the conjugations.

The more you practice, the better you will become. Verbs can be a challenge to the learner, but in your "***Building Block***," you can conjugate regular verbs, in the present tense, quickly and easily! Draw a window with the four sections and practice. Study Diagrams 3, 4, 5 and 6 to review how to correctly add the correct ending to the stem of each verb. Pay special attention to the endings, **AR**, **ER** and **IR**.

Some examples of regular (unconjugated) verbs:

Arrestar (To Arrest)
Abrir (To Open)
Acabar (To Complete)
Agradar (To Please)
Andar (To Walk)
Ayudar (To Help)
Buscar (To Seek)
Certificar (To Certify)
Escuchar (To Listen)
Matar (To Kill)
Responder (To Respond)
Terminar (To End)

Abrazar (To Hug)
Absolver (To Aquit)
Aceptar (To Accept)
Amar (To Love)
Asistir (To Assit)
Beber (To Drink)
Cantar (To Sing)
Cortar (To Cut)
Invitar (To Invite)
Recibir (To Receive)
Subir (To Climb)
Cuidar (To Guard/watch over)

EXAMPLE: ARRESTAR –TO ARREST (<u>arrest</u> is the stem and <u>ar</u> is the ending)

SINGLE   **PLURAL**

SINGLE	PLURAL
Yo – Arrest**o**	Nosotros(as) – Arrest**amos**
Usted – Arrest**a** Él – Arrest**a** Ella – Arrest**a**	Ustedes – Arrest**an** Ellos – Arrest**an** Ellas – Arrest**an**

Diagram #7

LET'S PRACTICE:

SINGLE   **PLURAL**

SINGLE	PLURAL
Yo	Nostotros/as
Usted Él Ella	Ustedes Ellos Ellas

SINGULAR	**PLURAL**
Yo	Nosotros/as
Usted Él Ella	Ustedes Ellos Ellas

SINGULAR	**PLURAL**
Yo	Nosotros/as
Usted Él Ella	Ustedes Ellos Ellas

Below, you will find a list of verbs that are commonly used in law enforcement. Of course, these are not inclusive to all of the verbs, but, are a great start. Take the time to look up these verbs either in a Spanish verb book or in a dictionary. Please pay close attention that many of these verbs will have multiple meanings. Remember, these verbs are in the "infinitive" form of the verb that means, every verb will start with "*to*."

Arrestar – to arrest
Andar
Abrir
Agarrar
Apagar
Asistir
Ayudar
Buscar
Beber
Callarse
Caminar
Cerrar
Comer
Conducir
Conocer
Contar
Contestar
Correr
Cortar
Dar
Decir
Dejar
Describir
Entrar
Entender
Escribir
Escuchar
Esperar
Estar

Explicar
Hacer
Hablar
Ir
Levantar
Leer
Llamar
Llegar
Llevar
Manejar
Mentir
Mirar
Mover
Necesitar
Parar
Pasar
Pedir
Pegar
Poner
Revisar
Robar
Saber
Salir
Ser
Tomar
Tener
Traer
Usar
Venir
Ver
Visitar

IRREGULAR VERBS

Great job! Now let's look at irregular verbs. Unfortunately in Spanish, you cannot always look at a verb and know if it will be regular or irregular. With practice, you will soon learn the regular and the irregular verbs.

If verbs follow the set endings for a particular tense, like **Hablar**, they are said to be 'regular.' If they do not, they are said to be, irregular. Moreover, there are very irregular verbs like, *ir* (to go), and *ser* (to be).

So what exactly does this mean for me when speaking Spanish? Funny you should ask. Let's take a look at some irregular verbs. An irregular verb changes throughout the entire conjugation. Each irregular verb is unique to its own conjugation, and the only way to know, is to learn them and practice them. The following irregular verbs are in the ***present tense***, and we will follow the same "***Building Block***" conjugation format and with the subject pronouns.

NOTES:

Cerrar (To Close)

Now you would think since this verb ends in "**ar**" it would be a regular verb, not so easy.

The stem changes, let's look:

SINGULAR	PLURAL
Yo - *Cierro*	Nosotros (as) - *Ceramos*
Usted - *Cierra* Él - *Cierra* Ella - *Cierra*	Usteded – *Cierran* Ellos - *Cierran* Ellas - *Cierran*

Diagram #8

Let's look at another irregular verb:

Tener (To Have)

Pay close attention to how the stem changes two times……

SINGULAR	PLURAL
Yo - *Tengo*	Nosotros(as) – *Tenemos*
Usted - *Tiene* Él - *Tiene* Ella - *Tiene*	Ustedes – *Tienen* Ellos - *Tienen* Ellas - *Tienen*

Diagram #9

Now let us examine three very strange irregular verbs that are used in every conversation:

Ir (To Go)

SINGULAR   **PLURAL**

Yo – *Voy*	Nosotros(as) – **Vamos**
Usted – *Va* Él – *Va* Ella – *Va*	Ustedes - *Van* Ellos - *Van* Ellas - *Van*

Diagram # 10

Ser (To Be – permanent state of being)

SINGULAR   **PLURAL**

Yo – *Soy*	Nosotros(as) - *Somos*
Usted – *Es* Él – *Es* Ella - *Es*	Ustedes – *Son* Ellos – *Son* Ellas - *Son*

Diagram #11

Estar (To Be – temporary state of being)

SINGULAR	PLURAL
Yo - *Estoy*	Nosotros(as) - *Estamos*
Usted - *Esta* Él – *Esta* Ella – *Esta*	Ustedes - *Estan* Ellos – *Estan* Ellas - *Estan*

Diagram #12

As you can tell by now, there is no rhyme or reason in how irregular verbs are conjugated. Fortunately, there are not many irregular verbs in the Spanish language. You will need to practice your irregular verbs more than regular verbs and you need to commit them to memory!

PAST TENSE (PRETERIT)

And now, let's tackle the past tense. There are many ways to express the past tense in Spanish; however we will address the simplest format.

For regular verbs, there is a simple format used throughout. We will still use the ***"Building Block"*** of verb conjugation however, in this section we will add the correct ending to the verb, apply the ending to the correct window section and bingo, we have the past tense for regular verbs.

In the past tense (preterit – *el pretérito*), for regular verbs, your conjugations follow the same basic format as present tense verbs, following the **ar, er, ir** endings. Let's take a look:

Let us try the verb, *Hablar* (To Speak)

SINGULAR	**PLURAL**
Yo - *Hablé*	Nosotros(as) - *Hablamos*
Usted - *Habló* Él - *Habló* Ella - *Habló*	Ustedes – *Hablaron* Ellos – *Hablaron* Ellas - *Hablaron*

Diagram #13

So, the verb translates to:

Hablé *(ah-bleh)*, means – I spoke

Habló *(ah-blow)* means – You spoke, He spoke, She spoke, It spoke,

Hablamos *(ah-blah-mos)* means – We spoke

Hablaron *(ah-blah-rohn)* means - They all spoke, They spoke (men), They spoke (women)

Now, to complicate matters, look at the conjugation "***hablamos***." This form is the same in the present tense and in the past tense. Why you might ask? There are many unwritten rules to the language. So, what this means is, you the speaker, and the person with whom you are speaking with, will understand what is being said is in the past tense, or the present tense, by the content of the conversation. Further, if you recall in the section concerning the written accent mark, please remember when a vowel has an accent mark above it, you must stress that vowel just a little bit more than the other vowels. Take for example the verb "HABLAR – To Speak.

In present tense, Yo hablo means – I SPEAK. In the past tense Usted, Él or Ella habló, means you, he or she spoke. The only difference between the two conjugated verbs is the accent mark over the letter "o." In written form this allows the reader to see this verb is in the past tense and to the listener, you would need to stress the vowel allowing the listener to hear the stress on the vowel. This will take some practice in verbal form.

Now let us look at an "**ER**" regular verb in the past tense:

Comer (To Eat)
Use the "***Building Block***" as above (diagram #1)

SINGULAR	PLURAL
Yo - *Comí*	Nosotros(as) - *Comimos*
Usted - *Comió* Él - *Comió* Ella - *Comió*	Ustedes – *Comieron* Ellos – *Comieron* Ellas - *Comieron*

Diagram #14

This verb then translates to:

Comí *(koh-me)* means – I ate

Comió *(koh-me-oh)* means – You ate, He ate, She ate, It ate

Comimos *(koh-me-mohs)* means – We ate

Comieron *(koh-me-eh-rohn)* means – They All ate, They (men) ate, They (women) ate

Now let's do an "**IR**" regular verb:

Vivir (To Live)

SINGULAR	PLURAL
Yo - *Viví*	Nosotros(as) – *Vivimos*
Usted - *Vivió* Él - *Vivió* Ella - *Vivió*	Ustedes - *Vivieron* Ellos – *Vivieron* Ellas – *Vivieron*

Diagram #15

Viví *(ve-ve)* means - I Lived

Vivió *(ve-ve-oh)* means – You lived, He lived, She lived, It lived

Vivimos *(ve-ve-mohs)* means – We lived

Vivieron *(ve-ve-eh-rohn)* means – They All lived, They (men) lived, They (women) lived

Finally, there is a common theme to the past tense for the regular verbs that end in "**er**" and in "**ir**." In the past tense, the verb conjugations for regular verbs have the same endings: **í, imos, ió,** and **ieron**. Again, the endings for the "we" form in "**er**" and "**ir**" verbs are the same as they are in present tense. It is how the verb is used in the conversation will determine if it is present tense or in past tense.

Try one more "**ir**" regular verb in the past tense:

Dormir (To Sleep)

SINGULAR	PLURAL
Yo - *Dormí*	Nosotros(as) - *Dormimos*
Usted - *Dormió* Él - *Dormió* Ella - *Dormió*	Ustedes – *Dormieron* Ellos – *Dormieron* Ellas - *Dormieron*

Diagram #16

Dormí *(dohr-me)* means – I slept

Dormió *(dohr-me-oh)* means – You slept, He slept, She slept, It slept

Dormimos *(dohr-me-mohs)* means – We slept

Dormieron *(dohr-me-eh-rohn)* means – They All slept, They (men) slept, They (women) slept

With irregular verbs, there are changes throughout each verb. Some verbs change the stem along with the ending, as other irregular verbs change entirely in spelling. Let us take a look at some irregular verbs in the past tense.

Ir (To Go)

SINGULAR	PLURAL
Yo - *Fui*	Nosotros/as - *Fuimos*
Usted - *Fue* Él – *Fue* Ella – *Fue*	Ustedes - *Fueron* Ellos – *Fueron* Ellas - *Fueron*

Diagram #17

Fui *(fu-ee)* means – I went

Fue *(fu-eeh)* means – You went, He went, She went, It went

Fuimos *(fu-ee-mohs)* means – We went

Fueron *(fu-ee-rohn)* means – They All went, They (men) went, They (women) went

Ser (To Be - permanent)

SINGULAR   **PLURAL**

Singular	Plural
Yo - *Fui*	Nosotros/as - *Fuimos*
Usted - *Fue* Él – *Fue* Ella – *Fue*	Ustedes – *Fueron* Ellos – *Fueron* Ellas – *Fueron*

Diagram #18

You may think I made a mistake in typing this book, sorry – no.

In Spanish the conjugations are the same for two different verbs, in the past tense, even though they mean different things.

Fui *(fu-ee)* means – I was

Fue *(fu-eeh)* means – You were, He was, She was, It was

Fuimos *(fu-ee-mohs)* means – We were

Fureon *(fu-ee-rohn)* means – They All were, They (men) were, They (women) were

So my friends, when you use these two verbs, you will need to be exact in how the verbs are being used in the context of the sentences and conversations.

Estar (To Be-temporary)

SINGULAR	PLURAL
Yo - *Estuve*	Nosotros/as – *Estuvimos*
Usted - *Estuvo* Él – *Estuvo* Ella – *Estuvo*	Ustedes – *Estuvieron* Ellos - *Estuvieron* Ellas - *Estuvieron*

Diagram #19

Estuve *(ehs-tu-veh)* means – I was

Estuvo *(ehs-tu-hoh)* means – You were, He was, She was, It was

Estuvimos *(ehs-tu-vee-mohs)* means – We Were

Estuvieron *(ehs-tu-vee-eh-rohn)* means – They All were, They (men) were, They (women) were

Since the irregular verbs are at times very difficult to try to conjugate, we encourage you to seek subject resources, such as verbs books, combining resources will enhance your Spanish concepts learning experience. Remember, the *"BUILDING BLOCKS"* is an easy format to conjugate verbs, past tense, present tense, and the future tense.

FUTURE TENSE

Wow, congratulations, you have done it. Now it is time to look at the future tense. There are several ways to say the future tense in Spanish. For this book, I will make this easy and painless. If you recall, the whole verb (before you conjugate the verb) is called the ***infinitive form***.

In this section, I will show you the easiest and the fastest way to say a simple future tense. A true form of a future tense is called, the "*Future*" tense, in this section we will work on an *Imperfect Future Tense*, in that, it is an action that is ***going*** to take place. Look at the following example:

"I am going to buy an apple."

In this sentence, the action is about to take place: Going to buy (an apple).

In Spanish, the easiest way to say a future action is conjugating the verb "**IR**" (an irregular verb) in the present indicative tense. Below is the "***Building Block***," for the irregular verb "**IR**," Remember, the four sections of the windows are the same as the regular verbs you already studied.

A Road Officer's Guide – Second Edition

IR – To Go

SINGULAR	**PLURAL**
Yo - *Voy*	Nosotros/as - *Vamos*
Usted – *Va* Él – *Va* Ella – *Va*	Ustedes – *Van* Ellos – *Van* Ellas – *Van*

Diagram #20

Once you have conjugated *IR*, as above, the below is the format you will use to construct your sentences:

Your sentences should resemble the following:

Yo Voy + a + infinitive verb + ending.

Va + a + infinitive verb + ending.
(remember with this conjugation, you need to **add** the appropriate pronouns)

Nosotros (as) Vamos + a + infinitive verb + ending.

Van + a + infinitive verb + ending.
(remember with this conjugation, you need to **add** the appropriate pronouns)

Example:

I am going to eat tacos.

Spanish:

Yo voy a comer tacos.

Yo voy = I am going

a = to

comer = (to) eat (THIS IS THE INFINITIVE VERB)

tacos = tacos.

Another example:

We are going to arrest the suspect.

Spanish:

Nosotros vamos a arrestar el sospechoso.

Nosotros vamos = We are going

a = to

arrestar = (to) arrest (THIS IS THE INFINITIVE VERB)

el sospechoso = the suspect.

Another Example:

They are going to search your car.
Spanish:

Ellos van a registrar su carro.

Ellos = They

van = are going

a = to

registrar = (to) search (THIS IS THE INFINITIVE VERB)

su = your

carro = car

Exercises:

Translate the following sentences into Spanish:

1.)   I am going to buy candy.

2.)   We are going to the beach.

3.)   He is going to rob a bank.

4.)   She is going to kill a man.

5.)   They are going to steal the money.

6.)   You are going to go to jail.

7.)   I am going to search your clothes.

8.)   We are going to search your car.

9.)   They are going to take your telephone.

COGNATES

Cognates are words that have a similar pronunciation and spelling in English and in Spanish, and frequently have the same meaning. There are many cognates shared by both languages. Many of them are words of Latin or Greek origin that have prefixes or suffixes derived from these ancient languages. I have gathered some brief examples related to work in law enforcement, but they are by no means exclusive. Be aware that the spelling will vary, but the meaning is generally the same. Following is a short list of common cognates.

Absurd - **absurdo** *(ahb-surh-doh)*
Accident - **accidente** *(ahk-see-dehn-the)*
Adverse - **adverso** *(adh-verh-soh)*
Agent - **agente** *(ah-hehn-teh)*
Agresssor - **aggressor** *(ah-grehs-sor)*
Adult - **adulto** *(ah-duhl-toh)*
Airplane - **avión** *(ah-vee-ohn)*
Arrogant **arrogante** *(ahr-roh-gahn-teh)*
Ambulance - **ambulancia** *(ahm-boo-lahn-see-ah)*
Concept - **concepto** *(kohn-cehp-toh)*
Agressive - **agresivo** *(ah-grehs-ee-voh)*
Alphabet - **alfabeto** *(ahl-fah-beh-toh)*
Air - **aire** *(eye-reh)*
Article - **artículo** *(arh-tee-kuh-low)*
Automobile - **automóvil** *(ah-ooh-toh-mo-vill)*
Basic - **básico** *(bah-see-koh)*
Bank - **banco** *(bahn-koh)*
Biology - **biología** *(bee-oh-loh-he-ah)*
Calendar - **calendario** *(kah-lehn-dahr-ee-oh)*
Candidate - **candidato** *(kahn-dee-dah-toh)*
Class - **clase** *(klah-say)*
Character - **carácter** *(cahr-ahk-tehr)*
Company - **compañía** *(kohm-pah-nee-ya)*
Cooperate - **cooperar** *(koh-oh-peh-rarh)*
Complex - **complejo** *(kohm-pleh-hoh)*
Cablegram- **cablegrama** *(kah-bleh-grah-mah)*
Confidence - **confianza** *(kohn-feh-ahn sah)*
Cause - **causa** *(cow-sah)*
Contraband - **contrabando** *(kohn-trah-bahn-doh)*
Complete - **completo** *(kohm-pleh-toh)*
Crime - **crimen** *(krihm-ehn)*

CHAPTER TWO

NUMBERS, COLORS, HUMAN BODY & TIME

0……………………**cero** (*seh-roh*)

1……………..…..**uno** (*oo-noh*)

2……………………**dos** (*dohs*)

3……………………**tres** (*trehs*)

4……………………**cuatro** (*kwah-troh*)

5……………………**cinco** (*seen-koh*)

6……………………**seis** (*seh-ees*)

7……………………**siete** (*see-eh-teh*)

8……………………**ocho** (*oh-choh*)

9……………………**nueve** (*noo-eh-veh*)

10…………………..**diez** *(dee-ehs)*

11…………………..**once** *(ohn-say)*

12…………………..**doce** *(doh-say)*

13…………………..**trece** *(treh-say)*

14…………………..**catorce** *(kah-torh-say)*

15…………………..**quince** *(keen-say)*

16.......................**dieciséis** *(dee-ehs-ee-seh-ees)*

17.......................**diecisiete** *(dee-ehs-ee-see-eh-teh)*

18.......................**dieciocho** *(dee-ehs-ee-oh-choh)*

19.......................**diecinueve** *(dee-ehs-ee-noo-eh-veh)*

20.......................**veinte** *(vehn-teh)*

30.......................**treinta** *(treh-ehn-tah)*

40.......................**cuarenta** *(kwah-rehn-tah)*

50.......................**cincuenta** *(seen-kwen-tah)*

60.......................**sesenta** *(seh-sehn-tah)*

70.......................**setenta** *(seh-tehn-tah)*

80.......................**ochenta** *(oh-chehn-tah)*

90.......................**noventa** *(noh-vehn-tah)*

100......................**cien / (ciento)** *(see-ehn / see-ehn-toh)*

200......................**doscientos** *(dohs-see-ehn-tohs)*

300......................**trescientos** *(treh-see-ehn-tohs)*

400......................**cuatrocientos** *(kwah-troh-see-ehn-tohs)*

500......................**quinientos** *(kehn-ee-ehn-tohs)*

600......................**seiscientos** *(seh-ees-see-ehn-tohs)*

700......................**setecientos** *(seh-teh-see-ehn-tohs)*

800.....................**ochocientos** *(oh-choh-see-ehn-tohs)*

900.....................**novecientos** *(noh-veh-see-ehn-tohs)*

1,000...................**mil** *(meel)*

10,000..................**diez mil** *(dee-ehs-meel)*

100,000.................**cien mil** *(see-ehn-meel)*

1,000,000...............**un millón** *(uhn-mee-yohn)*

Just for your reference, dates of birth are generally given as **"day/month/year"** in most Spanish speaking countries. Moreover, in the American culture (United States of American), when we identify a year of birth, it is stated for example 1999, or through a simple breakdown, **19 / 99**. In many Spanish speaking countries, years of birth will be identified as an example: 1999 – mil novecientos noventa y nueve, or, One Thousand Nine Hundred Ninety Nine. Therefore, you will need to practice years of birth in the aforementioned format - one thousand nine hundred and the year.............

Now, how in the world do you express numbers such as twenty-three, fifty-seven, eighty-four and so on? Have no fear! It is very simple to express numbers between 21 and 99. Say for example you want to say 47 in Spanish, you would simply say *"cuarenta siete"* forty seven. Let's look at some other examples. You want to say 72 in Spanish, you would say, *"setenta dos."* One final example, to express 83 in Spanish all you need to do is to say – *"ochenta tres."*

All you have to do is to select the ordinal number, 20, 30, 40, 50 and so on and then simply add the number 1 thru 9 to the ordinal number to complete your number in Spanish. Finally, if the numbers are greater than one hundred (but before 200) you

MUST say *"ciento"* which basically means ***100 and something else.***

Examples: 127 - ***Ciento veinte y siete*** *(the letter "y" means and)*
182 - ***Ciento ochenta dos***
146 - ***Ciento cuarenta seis***

For numbers 200-900 the following rules apply:

Examples: 256 – **Doscientos cincuenta seis**
899 – **Ochocientos noventa nueve**
631 – **Seiscientos treinta uno**

For numbers over one thousand, simply say for example: 1,483; mil cuatrocientos ochenta tres; 2,017, dos mil diecisiete and a final example – 3,492, tres mil cuatrocientos noventa dos. Remember, after one thousand, simply say – 1000 –mil, 2000 – dos mil, 3,000 – tres mil, 4,000 cuatro mil and so on.

REVIEW:

The number 100 in Spanish is – "**cien**." and means exactly 100. For any number from 101 thru 199, you must use the word "**ciento**" followed by an ordinal number and the numbers following. The numbers 21 thru 29, you must insert the letter "**y**" between 20 and the following number, 21-29. The numbers 30-90 do not need the letter "**y**" inserted. From 201-999, simply use the hundred number, followed by whole number (20-90) and then the numbers either 1-9, if applicable.

CARDINAL NUMBERS

First.....................**primero** *(pree-meh-roh)*

Second..................**segundo** *(seh-goon-doh)*

Third.....................**tercero** *(tehr-seh-roh)*

Fourth...................**cuarto** *(cooh-arh-toh)*

Fifth......................**quinto** *(keen-toh)*

Sixth.....................**sexto** *(sehk-toh)*

Seventh................**séptimo** *(sehp-tee-moh)*

Eighth...................**octavo** *(ohk-tah-voh)*

Ninth....................**noveno** *(noh-vehn-noh)*

Tenth....................**décimo** *(deh-see-moh)*

COLORS

As you can see below, some of the colors have numerous words to describe the color. The first five listed colors are the same for whatever they are describing. The remaining colors will match to the gender of the noun or adjective they modify. For example the color blue: a blue shirt – una camisa azul. The color will be the same regardless of the gender of the word it modifies. Staring with the color black – negro or negra to the end of the colors, the color will match the gender of the word it modifies, for example: a black shirt – una camisa negra. Remember, throughout Spanish gender of the words are an important aspect of the language. Therefore, the words

MUST agree not only in number (singular or plural) but in word gender (masculine or feminine).

Blue	**azul** (*ah-sool*)
Brown	**café** (*kah-feh*)
Cream	**crema** (*kreh-mah*)
Green	**verde** (*vehr-deh*)
Grey	**gris** (*grees*)
Black	**negro, negra** (*neh-groh, neh-grah*)
White	**blanco, blanca** (*blahn-koh, blahn-kah*)
Orange	**naranja, anaranjado, anaranjada** (*nah-rahnhah, ah-nah-rahn-hah-doh, ah-nah-rahn-hah-dah*)
Purple	**morado, morada - violeta** (*moh-rah-doh, mohrah-dah - vee-oh-leh-tah*)
Red	**rojo, roja – colorado, colorada** (*roh-hoh, rohhah, koh-loh-rah-doh, koh-loh-rah-dah*)
Yellow	**amarillo, amarilla** (*ah-mah-ree-yoh, ah-mah-reeyah*)
Gold	**dorado, dorada, oro** (*doh-rah-doh, doh-rah-dah, oh-roh*)
Silver	**plateado, plateada, plata** (*plah-teh-ah-doh, plah-tehah-dah, plah-tah*)
Light color	**Color claro** (*koh-lohr klah-roh*)
Dark color	**Color oscuro** (*koh-lohr ohs-koo-roh*)

NOTES:

THE HUMAN BODY

ankles	**los tobillos** *(lohs toh-be-yohs)*
anus	**el ano** *(ehl ah-noh)*
arms	**los brazos** *(lohs brah-sos)*
back	**la espalda** *(lah ehs-pahl-dah)*
bald	**pelón/calvo** *(peh-lohn / cahl-voh)*
beard	**la barba** *(lah barh-bah)*
blood	**sangre** *(sahn-greh)*
bone	**el hueso** *(ehl oo-eh-soh)*
breasts	**los senos** *(lohs seh-nohs)*
buttocks	**las nalgas** *(lahs nahl-gahs)*
calves	**las pantorrillas** *(lahs pahn-tor-ree-yahs)*
cheeks	**las mejillas** *(lahs mee-he-yahs)*
chest	**el pecho** *(ehl peh-choh)*
chin	**la barbilla** *(lah barh-bee-yah)*

ears	**las orejas** *(lahs ohr-eh-hahs)*
elbow	**el codo** *(ehl koh-doh)*
eyes	**los ojos** *(lohs oh-hos)*
eye brows	**las cejas** *(lahs seh-hahs)*
face	**la cara** *(lah- kah-rah)*
fat	**gordo/a** *(gohr-doh / gohr-dah)*
feet	**los pies** *(lohs pee-ehs)*
fingernails	**las uñas de la mano** *(lahs uh-neh-yas deh lah mah-no)*
fingers	**los dedos** *(lohs deh-dohs)*
freckle	**la peca** *(lah peh-kah)*
foot	**el pie** *(ehl pee-eyh)*
forearm	**el antebrazo** *(ehl ahn-teh-brah-soh)*
forehead	**la frente** *(lah frehn-teh)*
hair	**el pelo / el cabello** *(ehl peh-loh /ehl kah-beh-yoh)*
hands	**las manos** *(lahs mah-nohs)*
head	**la cabeza** *(lah kah-bayh-sah)*

heart	**el corazón** *(ehl kohr-ah-sohn)*
knees	**las rodillas** *(lahs roh-deh-yahs)*
legs	**las piernas** *(lahs pee-ehr-nahs)*
lips	**los labios** *(lohs lah-bee-ohs)*
mouth	**la boca** *(lah boh-kah)*
muscle	**el músculo** *(ehl muhs-cooh-loh)*
mustache	**el bigote** *(ehl bee-goh-teh)*
nape (of neck)	**la nuca** *(lah nuh-kah)*
neck	**el cuello** *(ehl cooh-eh-yoh)*
nipple	**el pezón** *(ehl peh-sohn)*
nose	**la nariz** *(lah nah-reehz)*
penis	**el pene** *(ehl peh-neeh)*
ribs	**las costillas** *(lahs kohs-tee-yahs)*
scar	**la cicatriz** *(lah see-kah-trihz)*
short	**chaparro/a, bajo/a** *(chah-pah-roh – chah-pah-rah / bah-hoh – bah-hah)*

skinny	**flaco/a, delgado/a** *(flah-koh – flah-kah /dehl-gah-doh – dehl gah-dah)*
tall	**alto / alta** *(ahl-toh / ahl-tah)*
tattoo	**el tatuaje** *(ehl tah-too-ah-hey)*
teeth	**los dientes** *(lohs dee-ehn-tehs)*
toes	**los dedos del pie** *(lohs deh-dohs dehl pee-eh)*
tongue	**la lengua** *(lah lehn-guh-ah)*
shoulders	**los hombros** *(lohs ohm-brohs)*
stomach	**el estómago** *(ehl ehs-toh-mah-goh)*
vagina	**la vagina** *(lah vah-he-nah)*
waist	**la cintura** *(lah sehn-turh-ah)*
wrists	**las muñecas** *(lahs muh-neh-eh-kahs)*

HOW TO TELL TIME IN SPANISH

The verb **ser** ("to be") is used to tell time in Spanish. Basically, the 3rd person singular form **_"es"_** is used to express the idea that it is **one o'clock or one something**. The 3rd person plural form **_"son"_** **is used to express all other times from two o'clock until 12 o'clock,** either a.m. or p.m. Minutes can be stated simply by separating them from the hour using the letter "*y*," the word for "and" in Spanish. This format is followed when expressing an hour of time and minutes. **Es la una.** It is 1:00.

- **Es la una y dos.** It is 1:02.

- **Son las dos.** It is 2:00.

- **Son las cuatro.** It is 4:00.

- **Son las seis y siete.** It is 6:07.

- **Son las siete y diez.** It is 7:10.

- **Son las once y diecinueve.** It is 11:19.

To indicate the half hour, use ***media***, regardless of the hour. Use ***cuarto*** to indicate a quarter past the hour. Use ***tres cuartos*** to indicate ¾ of an hour, or simply put - a quarter till the hour.

- **Es la una y media**. It is 1:30.

- **Son las cuatro y media**. It is 4:30.

- **Es la una y cuarto**. It is 1:15.

- **Es la una y tres cuartos**. It is 1:45.

In a majority of the Spanish-speaking world, both 12-hour and 24-hour clocks are used, the latter being quite common in schedules, police, military and in the banking industry. There is no concept of "AM" and "PM" as is used in the majority of the world. To indicate time of day when using the 12-hour clock, the following is used to indicate the segments of time within a 24 hour period.

<u>de la mañana</u> - 0000 hours (midnight) until 1200 hours (noon)

<u>de la tarde</u> – 1200 hours (noon) until 1900 (7:00 p.m.) hours

de la noche - 1900 (7:00 p.m.) hours until 0000 (midnight) hours

> **Es medianoche.** It's midnight.

> **Son las siete y cuarto de la mañana.** It's 7:15 a.m. (It is 7:15 in the morning.)

> **Es mediodía.** It's noon.

> **Son las ocho y media de la noche.** It's 8:30 p.m. (It is eight and a half at night.)

> **Here are some other time-related examples that can be useful:** <u>Faltan</u> **cinco minutos para las tres.**

It is 2:55 (literally meaning: It is <u>missing</u> 5 minutes before 3). (This expression, "falta (one minute) or faltan (2 thru 59 minutes) can be used any hour of the day).

> **Son las tres y cuarto <u>en punto.</u>** It's 3:15 <u>exactly</u>.

- **Son las seis y media más o menos**. It's about 6:30 (more or less)

- **Salimos a las nueve**. We are leaving at 9:00.

- **Era la una. Eran los dos** (tres, cuatro, etc.). It was 1:00. It was 2:00 (3:00, 4:00, etc.).

- **Buenos días**. Good day, good morning.

- **Buenas tardes**. Good afternoon, good evening (until about 7:00 p.m.).

- **Buenas noches**. Good evening (relating to telling time, the hours of 7:00 p.m. until midnight; good night (as either a greeting or a farewell).

- **¿Qué hora es?** *(keh orh-ah-ehs)* What time is it?

- **¿Cuándo** *(cooh-ahn-doh)***...?** When...?

➤ **Despues** (*dehs-puh-ehs*)... After

➤ **Antes** (*ahn-tehs*).... Before

PRACTICE TELLING TIME

Write the correct time in Spanish using a complete sentence. Further, use the correct time frame to indicate time of day: *de la mañana , de la tarde or de la noche.*

3:00 P.M.

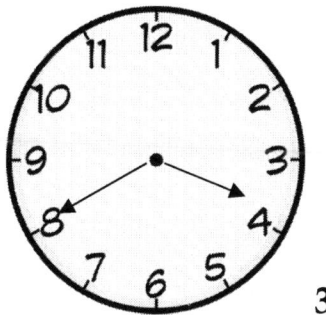

3:40 P.M.

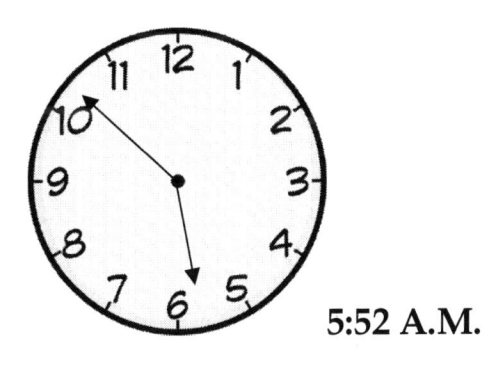

5:52 A.M.

NOTES:

CHAPTER THREE

DAYS OF THE WEEK, MONTHS OF THE YEAR & DIRECTIONS

In the Spanish language, the days of the week are capitalized. However, the months of the year are not capitalized and are in all lower case letters.

Monday…………………..**El Lunes** *(ehl luh-nehs)*

Tuesday…………………..**El Martes** *(ehl mahr-tehs)*

Wednesday………………**El Miércoles** *(ehl mee-ehr-koh-lehs)*

Thursday…………………**El Jueves** *(ehl huh-ee-vehs)*

Friday……………………**El Viernes** *(ehl vee-ehr-nehs)*

Saturday…………………**El Sábado** *(ehl sah-bah-doh)*

Sunday…………………...**El Domingo** *(ehl doh-mehn-goh)*

January…………………..**enero** *(eh-neh-roh)*

February………………….**febrero** *(feh-breh-roh)*

March…………………….**marzo** *(marh-soh)*

April……………………..**abril** *(ah-brihl)*

May………………………**mayo** *(mah-yoh)*

June............................**junio** *(hoo-nee-oh)*

July.............................**julio** *(hoo-lee-oh)*

August.........................**agosto** *(ah-gohs-toh)*

September....................**septiembre** *(sehp-tee-ehm-breh)*

October.......................**octubre** *(ohk-too-breh)*

November....................**noviembre** *(noh-vee-ehm-breh)*

December....................**diciembre** *(dee-see-ehm-breh)*

DIRECTIONS

MEASUREMENTS

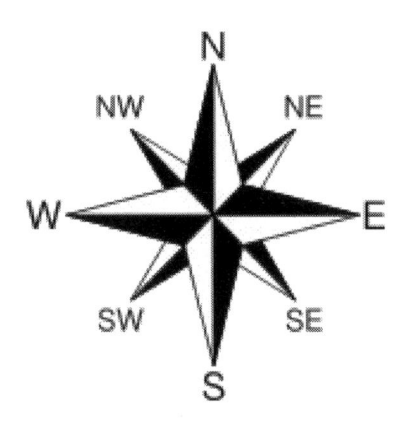

Being able to ask and understand directions is paramount in law enforcement. Not only knowing the directions of street, knowing the direction that a suspect may had fled is valuable information from witnesses or from victims.

North...................... **Norte** *(nohr-teh)*

South......................**Sur** *(suhr)*

East.......................**Este** *(ehs-teh)*

West......................**Oeste** *(oh-ehs-teh)*

Northeast................**Noreste** *(nohr-ehs-teh)*

Northwest...............**Noroeste** *(nohr-oo-ehs-teh)*

Southeast................**Sureste** *(suhr-ehs-teh)*

Southwest...............**Suroeste** *(suhr-oh-ehs-teh)*

In Mexico and many other countries, the usage of the metric system is utilized. Therefore, when you take someone into custody, be prepared when asking for physical information concerning height and weight to be given in the metric standards.

1 Centimeter equals 0.39 inches

26 Millimeters equals 1.02 inches

1 Meter equals 3.28 feet

1 Kilogram equals 2.2 pounds

CHAPTER FOUR

CLOTHING & SCARS / MARKS TATTOOS

Bandana......................**El pañuelo/La pañoleta** *(ehl pah-nyuh-ehl-oh/lah pah-nyoh-leh-tah)*

Ball cap......................**La Gorra** *(lah gohr-rah)*

Bathing Suit..................**El Traje de Baño** *(ehl trah-hay deh bah-nyoh)*

Belt..........................**El Cinturón** *(ehl sehn-tu-rohn)*

Blouse........................**La Blusa** *(lah bluh-sah)*

Body Piercing.................**Los Aretes del Cuerpo** *(lohs ah–reh-tehs dehl kwehr-poh)*

Boots.........................**Las Botas** *(lahs boh-tahs)*

Bra...........................**El Sostén** *(ehl soh-then)*

Bracelet......................**El Brazalete** *(ehl brah-sah-leh-tay)*

Clothing......................**La Ropa** *(lah roh-pah)*

Coins.........................**La Moneda** *(lah moh-neh-dah)*

Contacts (eyeware)............**Los Lentes de Contacto** *(lohs lehn-tehs deh kohn-tahk-tohs)*

Earrings......................**Los Aretes** *(lohs ah-reh-tehs)*

Eye Glasses	**Los Lentes (Anteojos)**	*(lohs lehn-tehs (ahn-tee-oh-hos)*
Gloves	**Los Guantes**	*(lohs gwah-tehs)*
Hat	**El Sombrero**	*(ehl sohm-brehr-oh)*
Jacket	**La Chaqueta**	*(lah chah-keh-tah)*
Jewelry	**Las Joyas**	*(lahs hoy-ahs)*
Knife	**La Navaja**	*(lah nah-vah-hah)*
Lighter	**El Encendedor**	*(ehl ehn-sehn-deh-dohr)*
Matches	**Los Fósforos**	*(lohs fohs-fohr-ohs)*
Nail Clippers	**El Cortaúñas**	*(ehl kohr-tah-uhn-yahs)*
Necklace	**El Collar**	*(ehl koh-yar)*
Overcoat	**El Abrigo**	*(ehl ah-breh-goh)*
Pajamas	**La Pijama**	*(lah pee-hahm-ah)*
Panties	**Las Bragas / calzones**	*(lahs brah-gahs / kahl-sohn-ehs)*
Pants	**Los Pantalones**	*(lohs pahn-tah-lohn-ehs)*
Purse	**La Bolsa/cartera**	*(lah bohl-sah / kahr-tehr-ah)*

Raincoat	**El Impermeable** *(ehl eem-pehr-meh-ah-bleh)*
Rings	**Los Anillos** *(lohs ah-nee-yohs)*
Sandals	**Las Sandalias** *(lahs sahn-dahl-ee-ahs)*
Shirt	**La Camisa** *(lah kah-me-sah)*
Shoes	**Los Zapatos** *(lohs sah-pah-tohs)*
Shorts	**Los Pantalones Cortos** *(lohs pahn-tah-lohn-es kohr tohs)*
Skirt	**La Falda** *(lah fahl-dah)*
Slip	**La Combinación** *(lah kohm-bee-nah-see-ohn)*
Slippers	**Las Zapatillas** *(lahs sah-pah-tee-yahs)*
Socks	**Las Medias** *(lahs meh-dee-ahs)*
Sport coat	**El Saco** *(ehl sah-koh)*
Suit	**El Traje** *(ehl trah-hay)*
Sunglasses	**Las Gafas** *(lahs gah-fahs)*
Sweater	**El Suéter** *(ehl sweh-tehr)*
T-Shirt	**La Playera/Camiseta** *(lah plah-yehr-ah / kah-me-seh-tah)*
Tennis shoes	**Los Tenis** *(lohs tehn-eehs)*

Underwear (mens/womens)....**La Ropa Interior** *(lah roh-pah ehn-tehr-ee-ohr)*

Uniform……………………..**El Uniforme** *(ehl oo-nee-fohr-meh)*

Vest……………………….**El Chaleco** *(ehl chah-leh-koh)*

Wallet……………………..**La Cartera / Billetera** *(lah kahr-tehr-ah / beh-yah-tehr-ah)*

Watch……………………..**El reloj** *(ehl reh-loh)*

Wig………………………..**La Peluca** *(lah pee-luh-kah)*

SCARS / MARKS / TATTOOS

As we know, the documentation of all scars, marks and tattoos are an invaluable asset to law enforcement. Just imagine how many Pedro Gonzalez's or any other name that there are in the world. The importance lies when questions are asked and you take the time to properly document every scar, mark and tattoo. We know that seems so redundant to do, especially if you work in a booking area. Just imagine how important that information may be in catching a cop killer if the only information that is known is a single tattoo - Farfetched? No, killers have been caught by the identity of a single tattoo. Please take the time and encourage arresting officers to do the same, the life they may save may be yours!

Do you have tattoos?
¿Tiene usted tatuajes?
(tee-ehn-eh oohs-tehd tah-too-ah-hays)

Where are they located (on your body)?
¿En qué parte (de su cuerpo)?
(ehn kay par-teh (deh suh kuh-ehr-poh)?)

What kind of tattoo is it?
¿Qué clase de tatuaje es?
(kay klah-seh deh tah-too-ah-hay ehs?)

What are the letters?
¿Qué significan las letras?
(kay seeg-nehf-feh-kahn lahs leh-trahs?)

Are they gang tattoos?
¿Son tatuajes de alguna pandilla?
(sohn tah-too-ah-hays deh ahl-guhn-ah pahn-deh-yah?)

Which gang?
¿De qué pandilla son?
(deh kay pahn-deh-yah sohn?)

Do you have birthmarks?
¿Tiene usted estigmas / marcas?
(tee-ehn-eh oohs-tehd ehs-tehg-mahs / marh-kahs?)

CHAPTER FIVE
TRAFFIC STOPS / FELONY STOPS

VEHICLE TYPES

COMMERCIAL VEHICLES /STREETS & BYWAYS

TRAFFIC CRASH INITIAL QUESTIONS

The following section is written in a concise manner. As you know when conducting a traffic stop, nothing is the same. The violations may be similar, but every stop has its own variables, time of day, weather, location, amount of present traffic and so on. I will highly encourage you to practice these words, statements and commands. Since there are so many different situations, I have grouped them into general stops. PLEASE, practice the traffic stop vocabulary and practice your felony stops in Spanish. There may not be time for a Spanish speaking officer to assist you. ***You do your job unique to you!*** Look through the following sentences and commands and make yourself cheat cards and keep them close - in your pocket, sun visor, door pocket, somewhere close whereby you can access them quickly. Please, practice this section.

Good morning sir (ma'm), how are you?
  Buenos días señor (señora), ¿cómo está? (*boo-eh-nohs dee-ahs seh-nyorh (seh-nyora) koh-moh ehs-stah*)

Do you know why I stopped you?
  ¿Sabe por qué lo paré? (*sah-beh pohr keh loh pah-reh*)

You have broken the law.
  Ha violado la ley (*ah vee-oh-lah-doh lah leh*)

I am officer......... **Soy oficial**........ *(soy oh-feh-see-ahl)*

ASKING FOR DOCUMENTS

Do you have...? **¿Tiene ...** *(tee-eh-neh...)*

...driver's license **la licencia de manejar?**
(lah lee-sehn-see-ah deh mah-neh-har)

...registration **el registro** *(ehl reh-hees-troh)*

...proof of ownership **el documento de propiedad**
(ehl doh-koo-mehn-toh deh proh-pee-eh-dahd)

...proof of insurance **la prueba del seguro**
(lah proo-eh-bah dehl seh-goo-roh)

EXAMPLES OF VIOLATIONS

You went through a red light **Pasó por la luz roja** *(pah-soh pohr lah loos rroh-hah)*

You were driving very fast **Iba manejando muy rapido** *(ee-bah mah-neh-hahn-doh moo-ee rrah-pee-doh)*

You were racing **Iba corriendo** *(ee-bah coh-ree-ehn-doh)*

You did not signal **No puso las señales** *(noh poo-soh lahs seh-nyah-lehs)*

You did not yield	**No cedió el paso** (*noh seh-dee-oh ehl pah-soh*)
You did not obey the sign	**No obedeció el signo** (*noh oh-beh-deh-see-oh ehl seeg-noh*)
You made an illegal turn	**Hizo una vuelta ilegal** (*ee-soh oo-nah voo-ehl-tah ee-leh-gahl*)
You were following too closely	**Estaba siguiendo demasiado cerca** (*ehs-tah-bah see-guee-ehn-doh deh-mah-see-ah-doh serh-kah*)
You crossed the line	**Cruzó la línea** (*kroo-soh lah lee-neh-ah*)
You almost crashed	**Casi chocó** (*kah-see choh-koh*)
You almost hit it	**Casi le pegó** (*kah-see leh peh-goh*)
You didn't have the right of way	**No tenía el derecho de vía** (*noh teh-nee-ah ehl deh-reh-choh deh vee-ah*)
You were swerving	**Estaba zigzagueando** (*ehs-tah-bah seeg-sah-geh-ahn-doh*)
I observed you on radar	**Lo observé en radar** (*loh ohb-serh-veh ehn rrah-dahr*)
You were driving at ___ mph	**Iba a ___ millas por hora** (*ee-bah ah ___ mee-yahs pohr oh-rah*)

Do you know the speed limit?	**¿Sabe cuál es el límite de velocidad?** (*sah-beh koo-ahl ehs ehl lee-mee-teh deh veh-loh see-dahd*)
Do you know how fast you were driving?	**¿Sabe a qué velocidad iba manejando?** (*sah-beh ah keh veh-loh-see-dahd ee-bah mah-neh-han-doh*)
Your visibility is obstructed	**Su visibilidad está obstruida** (*soo vee-see-bee-lee-dahd ehs-tah ohbs-troo-ee-dah*)
You were driving too slowly	**Iba manejando demasiado lento** (*ee-bah mah-neh-hahn-doh deh-mah-see-ah-dohlehn-toh*)
You were going against traffic	**Iba manejando contra el tráfico** (*ee-bah mah-neh-hahn-doh kohn trah ehl trah-fee-koh*)
You were cutting the corner	**Iba recortando la esquina** (*ee-bah re-kohr-tahn-doh lah ehs-kee-nah*)
You have too many passengers	**Tiene demasiados pasajeros** (*tee-eh-neh deh-mah-see-ah-dohs pah-sah-heh-rohs*)
You were in the car pool lane	**Iba por la pista de transporte en grupo** (*ee-bah pohr lah pees-tah deh trahns-pohr-teh ehn groo-poh*)

You were backing up	**Iba retrocediendo** (*ee-bah reh-troh-seh-dee-ehn-doh*)
You were littering	**Estaba tirando basura** (*ehs-tah-bah tee-rahn-doh bah-soo-rah*)
You must slow down	**Debe disminuir la velocidad** (*deh-beh dees-mee-noo-eer lah veh-loh-see-dahd*)

YOU DIDN'T STOP FOR	*NO SE DETUVO PARA....* (*noh seh deh-too-voh pah-rah...*)
...police car	**el carro de policía** (*ehl kah-rroh deh poh-lee-see-ah*)
...ambulance	**la ambulancia** (*lah ahm boo-lahn-see-ah*)
...fire truck	**el camión de bomberos** (*ehl kah-mee-ohn deh bohm-beh-rohs*)
...school bus	**el autobús escolar** (*ehl ow-toh-boos ehs-koh-lahr*)
...siren	**la sirena** (*lah see-reh-nah*)
...red lights	**las luces rojas** (*lahs loo-cehs rroh-hahs*)
...blue lights	**las luces azules** (*lahs loo-cehs ah-suhl-ehs*)
...pedestrian	**el peatón** (*ehl peh-ah-tohn*)
...train	**el tren** (*ehl trehn*)

You Cannot...	*No Puede* (*noh poo-eh-deh...*)
...drive without a license	**manejar sin licencia** (*mah-neh-hahr seen lee-sehn-see-ah*)
...drive without an adult	**manejar sin un adulto** (*mah-neh-hahr seen oon ah-dool-toh*)
...make a U-turn	**darse vuelta en U** (*dahr-seh voo-ehl-tah ehn oo*)
...pass on the right	**pasar por la derecha** (*pah-sahr pohr lah deh-reh-chah*)
...change lanes that way	**cambiar pistas así** (*kahm-bee-ahr pees-tahs ah-see*)
...turn here	**darse vuelta aquí** (*dahr-seh voo-ehl-tah ah-kee*)
...stop there	**parar ahí** (*pah-rarh- ah-ee*)
...back up	**retroceder** (*reh-troh-seh-dehr*)
...block traffic	**obstruir el tráfico** (*ohbs-troo-eer ehl trah-fee-koh*)
...tow another car	**remolcar otro carro** (*reh-mohl-kahr oh troh kah-rroh*)

INTERVIEW OF THE DRIVER

Are you the owner?	**¿Es usted el dueño?** (*ehs osted ehl doo-eh-nyoh*)

Do you have any other IDs?	**¿Tiene más pruebas de identificación?** *(tee-eh-neh mahs proo-eh-bahs deh ee-dehn-tee-fee-kah-see-ohn)*
Is this information correct?	**¿Es correcta esta información?** *(ehs koh-rrehk-tah ehs-tah een-fohr-mah-see-ohn)*
Where are you going?	**¿Adónde va?** *(ah-dohn-deh-vah)*
How long have you been driving?	**¿Por cuánto tiempo ha estado manejando?** *(pohr kwan-toh tee-ehm-poh ah ehs-tah-doh mah-neh-hahn-doh)*
Your license is expired	**Su licencia ha expirado** *(soo lee-sehn-see-ah ah ex-pee-rah-doh)*
Your plates have expired	**Sus placas han expirado** *(soos plah-kahs ahn ex-pee-rah-doh)*
There is a problem	**Hay una problema** *(ah-ee oon-nah proh-bleh-mah)*
Your license was revoked	**Su licencia fué cancelada** *(soo lee-sehn-see-ah foo-eh kahn-seh-lah-dah)*
You are too young to drive	**Es demasiado joven para manejar** *(ehs deh-mah-see-ah-doh hoh-vehn pah-rah mah-neh-har)*

Are there weapons in the car? ¿**Hay armas en el carro?** (*eye arh-mahs ehn ehl kah-rroh*)

Are there drugs in the car? ¿**Hay drogas en el carro?** (*eye droh-gahs ehn ehl kah-rroh*)

STREET AND BYWAYS

Avenue..........................**Avenida** (*ah-veh-neeh-dah*)

Alley.............................**Callejón** (*kah-yeh-hohn*)

Block............................**Manzana** (*mahn-zah-nah*)

Circle............................**Circulo** (*seer-koo-loh*)

Dead End......................**Sin Salida** (*seen sah-leh-dah*)

Freeway........................**Autopista** (*ah-oo-toh pees-tah*)

Highway.......................**Carretera** (*kah-re-teh-rah*)

Lane..............................**Carril** (*kah-rreel*)

One Way.......................**De sentido único** (*deh sehn-tee-doh uh-nee-koh*)

Road..............................**Camino** (*kah-mee-noh*)

Street.............................**Calle** (*kah-yeh*)

Square...........................**Plaza** (*plah-sah*)

Two-lane highway..........**Carretera de dos carriles** (*kah-re-teh-rah deh dohs kah-reel-ehs*)

FELONY CAR STOP

When conducting a traffic stop that results in a felony stop, your safety is absolute! I highly encourage you to practice this section and become very familiar with the commands. The more you practice, the easier it will be to give the commands in a calm but yet authoritative voice.

The following commands are written in a manner in which a felony traffic stop may occur. Nothing goes to plan. Please rearrange the commands to fit your style of a felony stop. Since felony traffic stops are volatile in nature, give the commands in English as well as in Spanish. This way, you can always testify that you offered your best effort to remove the occupants of the vehicle in a safe manner utilizing two languages. Remember, don't rely on only English speakers that are stopped, give the commands in English, then in Spanish, loudly and concisely.

Police!	**Policía!** *(poh-leh-see-ah)*
Driver, with your left hand, lower your window	**Chofer, con la mano izquierda, baje la ventana** *(choh-fehr, kohn lah mah-no ees-kee-ehr-dah, bah-hay lah vehn-tah-nah)*
Driver, with your left hand, turn off the motor	**Chofer, con la mano izquierda, apague el motor** *(choh-fehr, kohn lah mah-no ees-kee-ehr-dah, ah-pah-gay ehl moh-tohr)*

Driver, with your left hand, pull the keys out

Chofer, con la mano izquierda, saque las llaves
choh-fehr, kohn lah mah-no ees-kee-ehr-dah, sah-kay lahs yah-vehs)

Driver, put your hands and the keys out the window and drop the keys

Chofer, ponga las manos y las llaves afuera de la ventana, suelte las llaves (*choh-fehr, pohn-gah lahs mah-nohs ee lahs yah-vehs ah-fu-eh-rah deh lah vehn-tah-nah, soo-ehl-teh lahs yah-vehs*)

Driver, with your left hand, open the door and get out of the car slowly

Chofer, con la mano izquierda, abra la puerta, salga del carro, despacio (*choh-fehr, kohn lah mah-no ees-kee-ehr-dah, ah-brah lah poo-ehr-tah, sahl-gah dehl kar-roh, dehs-pah-see-oh*)

Slowly, get out of the car

Despacio, salga del carro (*dehs-pah-see-oh, sahl-gah dehl kah-rroh)*

Everyone in the car, put your hands up	**Todo el mundo en el carro, pongan las manos arriba** (*toh-doh ehl muhn-doh ehn ehl kah-rroh, pohn-gahn lahs mah-nohs ah-rree-bah*)
Put your hands on your head	**Pongan las manos en la cabeza** (*pohn-gahn lahs mah-nohs ehn lah kah-beh-sah*)
Don't move	**No se mueva** (*no seh moo-eh-vah*)
Put you hands up (higher)	**Ponga las manos más arriba** (*pohn-gah lahs mah-nohs mahs ah-ree-bah*)
Slowly turn around	**Dése vuelta despacio** (*deh-seh voo-ehl-tah dehs-pah-see-oh*)
Stop! Drop the weapon or I'll shoot	**Alto! Suelte el arma o disparo** (*ahl-toh! soo-ehl-teh ehl arh-mah oh dees-pah-roh*)
Slowly, walk toward my voice	**Despacio, camine hacia mi voz** (*dehs-pah-see-oh, kah-me-neh ah-see-ah mee vohs*)
Stop	**Alto** (*ahl-toh*)
Kneel down, slowly	**De rodillas, despacio** (*deh roh-dee-yahs, dehs-pah-see-oh*)

Cross your feet	**Cruce los pies** (*kroo-say lohs pee-ehs*)
Lie down (face down)	**Acuéstese boca abajo** (*ah-koo-ehs-teh-say boh-kah ah-bah-ho*)
Arms out	**Brazos afuera** (*brah-sohs ah-foo-eh-rah*)
Palms up	**Palmas arriba** (*pahl-mahs ah-ree-bah*)
Put your hands on your back	**Ponga las manos en la espalda** (*pohn-gah lahs mah-nohs ehn lah ehs-pahl-dah*)
Turn your head to the left/right	**Voltee la cabeza a la izquierda/derecho** (*vohl-teh eh lah kah-beh-sah ah lah ees-kee-ehr-dah/deh-reh-chah*)
Don't move	**No se mueva** (*no say moo-eh-vah*)
Do you have any weapons?	**¿Tiene armas?** (*tee-ehn-eh ahr-mahs*)
You are under arrest.	**Está arrestado** (*eh-stah ah-rresh-tah-doh*)
Put your hands up, slowly	**Manos arriba, despacio** (*mah-nohs ah-rree-bah, dehs-pah-see-oh*)

Put your hands on your head and interlace your fingers	**Ponga las manos en la cabeza y entrelace los dedos** (*pohn-gah lahs mah-nohs ehn lah kah-beh-sah ee ehn-treh-lah-say lohs deh-dohs*)
Cross your feet	**Cruce los pies** (*kroo-say lohs pee-ehs*)
Passenger in the front	**Pasajero del frente** (*pah-sah-heh-roh dehl frehn-teh*)
Passenger in the back seat/right side	**Pasajero de atrás, a la derecha** (*pah-sah-heh-roh day ah-trahs, ah lah deh-reh-cha*)
Passenger, in the back seat/middle	**Pasajero de atrás, en el medio** (*pah-sah-heh-roh day ah-trahs, ehn ehl meh-dee-oh*)
Passenger in the back seat/left side	**Pasajero de atrás, a la izquierda** (*pah-sah-heh-ro day ah-trahs, ah la ees-kee-ehr-dah*)
With your left hand, open the door	**Con la mano izquierda, abra la puerta** (*kohn lah mah-noh ehs-keh-ehr-dah, ah-brah lah poo-ehr-tah*)

Once you have the driver under control and you begin to remove all other occupants, go back to the previous commands in this section and repeat until each occupant has been removed and secured.

DUI INFORMATION

Sir/Miss, your driver's license, please.
(Señor/señora, su licencia, por favor.)
(see-nohr/see-nohr-ah, suh lee-cehn-see-ah, pohr fah-vohr)

Sir/Miss, your name / address / d.o.b.
(Señor/señora, su nombre/dirección/fecha de nacimiento.)
(see-nohr/see-nohr-ah, suh nohm-breh/ dee-rehk-see-ohn feeh-chah day nah-see-me-ehn-toh)

Sir,/Miss you were stopped because you were swerving.
(Señor/señora, usted fue detenido por en zigzagueando.)
(see-nohr/see-nohr-ah, ooh-stehd foo-eh day-tehn-eh-doh pohr ehn seeg-sah-geh-ahn-doh)

Sir/Miss, have you had any alcoholic beverages?
(¿Señor/señora, ha tomado bebidas alcoholicas?)
(see-nohr/see-nohr-ah, ah toh-mah-doh bay-bee-dahs ahl-kohl-ee-kahs)

Sir/Miss, what did you drink?
(¿Señor/señora, qué bebió?)
(see-nohr/see-nohr-ah, kay beh-bee-oh)

Sir/Miss, how much did you drink?
(¿Señor/señora, qué tanto bebió?)
(see-nohr/see-nohr-ah, kay tahn-toh beh-bee-oh)

Sir/Miss, please get out of the car.
(Señor/señora, salga del carro, por favor.)
(see-nohr/see-nohr-ah,, sahl-gah dehl kah-rroh pohr fah-vohr)

Sir/Miss, when did you start drinking?
(¿Señor/señora, cuándo comensó a beber?)
(see-nohr/see-nohr-ah, koo-ahn-doh koh-mehn-soh ah bay-behr)

Where?
(¿Dónde?)
(dohn-day)

Sir/Miss, when did you stop drinking?
(¿Señor/señora, cuándo dejo de beber?)
(see-nohr/see-nohr-ah, koo-ahn-doh day-ho day bay-behr)

Sir/Miss, where were you going?
(¿Señor/señora, dónde iba?)
(see-nohr/see-nohr-ah, dohn-day-eeh-bah)

Sir/Miss, where were you coming from?
(¿Señor/señora, de dónde venía?)
(see-nohr/see-nohr-ah, day dohn-day vay-neh-ah)

When did you last eat?
(¿Cuándo fue la última vez que comió?)
(koo-ahn-doh foo-eh lah uhl-tee-mah vehs kay koh-mee-oh)

What did you eat?
(¿Qué comió?)
(kay koh-mee-oh)

Are you taking any kind of medication?
(¿Requiere medicina?)
(ree-kee-erh-ee meh-dee-see-nah)

What for?
(¿Para qué?)
(pah-rrah kay)

When did you last take medication?
(¿Cuándo fue la ultima vez qué tomó medicina?)
(koo-ahn-doh foo-eh lah uhl-tee-mah vehs kay toh-moh meh-dee-see-nah)

What is the time now?
(¿Qué hora es?)
(kay ohr-ah-ehs)

What is today's date?
(¿Cuál es la fecha de hoy?)
(koo-ahl ehs lah fee-chah day hohy)

What day of the week is it?
(¿Qué dia de semana es?)
(kay dee-ah day say-mah-na ehs)

ALCOHOL AND OPEN CONTAINERS

Alcohol..............................**Alcohol** *(ahl-koh-ohl)*

Beer..................................**Cerveza** *(cehr-veh-sah)*

Bottle................................**Botella** *(boh-tay-yah)*

Can...................................**Lata** *(lah-tah)*

Container..........................**Envase** *(ehn-vah-say)*

Drunk (person)...............	**Borracho(a)** *(bohr-'rah-choh (ah)*
Illegal........................	**Ilegal** *(eh-leh-gahl)*
Liquor.........................	**Licor** *(leh-kohr)*
Possession....................	**Posesión** *(poh-sehs-ee-yohn)*
Six Pack......................	**Un Seis** *(uhn 'seeh-ees)*
Twelve Pack..................	**Un Doce** *(uhn 'doh-seh)*
Underage.....................	**Menor de edad** *(meh-nohr deh eh-dahd)*
Have you been drinking liquor?	**¿Ha estado tomando licor?** *(ah ehs-tah-doh toh-mahn-doh leh-kohr)*
It is unlawful to have an open container in your car.	**Es ilegal tener un envase abierto (licor) (alcohol) en el carro.** *(ehs eh-leh-gahl teh-nehr uhn enn-vah-say ah-beh-ehr-toh (leh-kohr)(ahl-koh-ohl) ehn ehl 'kah-roh)*

It is unlawful for an underage person to have alcohol.	**Es ilegal que un menor de edad a tenga alcohol.** *(ehs eh-leh-gahl queh uhn meh-nohr deh eh-dahd ah teh-gah ahl-koh-ohl)*
You are under arrest for possession of alcohol.	**Esta arrestado por posesión de alcohol.** *(eh-stah ah-'rehs-stah-doh pohr poh-sehs-e-yohn deh ahl-koh-ohl)*
I am taking the alcohol for evidence.	**Estoy tomando el alcohol por evidencia.** *(esh-tohy toh-mahn-doh ehl ahl-koh-ohl pohr eh-veeh-dehn-see-yah)*
Your parents are coming for you.	**Sus padres vienen por usted.** *(suhs pah-drehs veh-ehn-nehn pohr uh-stehd)*

PERFORMANCE TEST

Will you do a roadside examine to determine how much alcohol is in your body?

¿Hará un examen de carretera para determinar cuánto alcohol hay en su cuerpo? *(ah-rah uhn ehs-ah-mehn day kah-rreh-tehr-ah pah-rah day-tahr-mee-nahr koo-ahn-toh ahl-koh-ahl eye ehn suh koo-ehr-poh)*

I am going to give you..
(Yo voy a darle…)
(yoh voh-ah dahr-leh…)

A test…
(Un examen de….)
(uhn ehk-ah-mehn day)

Balance
(Equilibrio)
(ee-kee-lee-bree-oh)

Coordination
(Coordinación)
(koh-orh-dee-nah-see-ohn)

Urine
(Orina)
(oh-ree-nah)

Blood
(Sangre)
(sahn-greh)

Breath
(Aliento)
(ah-lee-ehn-toh)

Sobriety
(Sobriedad)
(sobree-eh-dahd)

Sir, Ma'am recite the alphabet
(Señor/señora, recite el alfabeto.)
(see-nohr/see-nohr-ah, ray-cee-tay ehl ahl-fah-beh-toh)

Walking heel to toe in a straight line.
(Señor/señora, camine, el talon en frente del dedo del pie en línea recta)
(see-nohr/see-nohr-ah, kah-mee-neh, ehl tah-lohn ehn frehn-tay dehl day-doh dehl pee-eh ehn lee-nee-ah rehk-tah)

Follow the movement of this pen, eyes only, don't move the head.
(Señor/señora, siga el movimiento de la pluma con sus ojos, no mueva la cabeza.)
(see-nohr/see-nohr-ah, see-gah ehl moh-vee-mee-ehn-toh day lah pluh-mah kohn suhs oh-hohs, no moo-eh-vah lah kah-beh-sah)

Maintain your arms to your sides....
(Mantenga sus brazos al lado...)
(mahn-tehn-gah suhs brah-sos ahl lah-doh)

Place your feet together...
(Ponga sus pies juntos...)
(pohn-gah suhs pee-ehs huhn-tohs...)

Move your head backwards...
(Mueva su cabeza hacia atrás...)
(moo-eh-vah suh kah-beh-sah ah-see-ah ah-trahs....)

Without looking, touch your nose with your right first finger…
(Sin mirar, toca su nariz con su primer dedo derecho…)
(sihn mih-rahr, toh-kah suh nah-reehz kohn suh preh-mehr day-doh day-reh-choh)

Without looking, touch your nose with your left first finger…
(Sin mirar, toca su nariz con su primer dedo izquierdo…)*(sihn mih-rahr, toh-kah suh nah-reehz kohn suh preh-mehr day-doh eehs-keeh-ehr-doh…)*

Look at my eyes, now…
(Mire a mis ojos, ahorra…)
(mee-reh ah meehs oh-hohs, ah-ohrr-ah)

Raise your left leg….
(Levante su pierna izquierda…)
(lee-vahn-teh suh pee-erh-nah ees-kee-erh-dah….)

Raise your right leg…
(Levante su pierna derecha…)
(lee-vahn-the suh pee-ehr nah day-reh-chah)

Don't move….
(No se mueva…)
(noh say moo-eh-vah)

Sir/Miss, you are under arrest for driving while under the influence of alcohol/drugs.

(Señor/señora, esta arrestado por estar bajo la influencia de alcohol/drogas mientras que manejaba el carro.)
(see-nohr/see-nohr-ah, eh-stah ah-rrehs-tah-doh pohr eh-stahr bah-hoh lah ehn-flu-ehn-cee-ah day ahl-koh-ahl/droh-gahs mee-ehn-trahs kay mah-neh-hah-bah ehl kah-rroh)

VEHICLE TYPES

The Auto............. **El auto** (*ehl ah-ooh-toh*)

The Automobile..... **El automóvil** (*ehl ah-ooh-toh-moh-veel*)

New Model.......... **Modelo nuevo** (*moh-deh-loh noo-eh-voh*)

Old Model...........**Modelo viejo** (*moh-deh-loh vee-eh-hoh*)

The Bus...............**El autobús** (*ehl ah-ooh-toh-buhs*)

The Car...............**El coche, el carro** (*ehl koh-cheh, ehl kah-rroh*)

A Convertible........**Un convertible** (*oon kohn-verh-tee-blee*)

With Two Doors.....**Con dos puertas** (*kohn dohs poo-ehr-tahs*)

With Four Doors.... **Con cuatro puertas** (*kohn koo-ah-troh poo-ehr-tahs*)

Four by Four.........**Cuatro por cuatro** (*koo-ah-troh pohr koo-ah-troh*)

The Bicycle..........**La bicicleta** (*lah bee-see-kleh-tah*)

A Motorcycle........ **Una motocicleta** (*oo-nah moh-toh-see-kleh-tah*)

A Moped............. **Una motoneta, Un ciclomotor** (*oo-nah moh-toh-neh-tah, oon seeh-kloh-moh-tohr*)

The Truck..............**El camión** (*ehl kah-mee-ohn*)

A Sports car..........**Un auto deportivo** (*oon auh-toh deh-por-tee-voh*)

The Tow Truck......**La grúa** (*lah groo-ah*)

A Traffic Crash......**Un accidente de tráfico** (*oon ahk-see-dehn-teh deh trah-fee-koh*)

Eye Witnesses......**Los testigos** (*lohs tehs-tee-gohs*)

Police Report.......**El informe policial** (*ehl een-fohr-meh poh-lee-see-ahl*)

TRAFFIC CRASH / INJURY QUESTIONS

Are you O.K. ? **¿Está bien?** (*ehs-tah bee-ehn*)

Calm down. **Cálmese.** (*kahl-meh-seh*)

What is your name? **¿Cómo se llama?** (*koh-moh seh yah-mah*)

Where do you hurt? **¿Dónde le duele?** (*dohn-deh leh doo-eh-leh*)

Are you hurt/injured? **¿Está lastimado/herido?** (*ehs-tah lahs-tee-mah-doh/eh-ree-doh*)

Show me the place. **Enséñeme el lugar** (*ehn-sehn-nyeh-meh ehl looh-gahr*)

Arms?	**¿Brazos?** (*brah-sohs*)
Back?	**¿Espalda?** (*ehs-pahl-dah*)
Head?	**¿Cabeza?** (*kah-beh-sah*)
Legs?	**¿Piernas?** (*pee-ehr-nahs*)
Ankles?	**¿Tobillos?** (*toh-bee-yoohs*)
Elbow?	**¿Codo?** (*koh-dohs*)
Fingers?	**¿Dedos?** (*deh-dohs*)
Foot?	**¿Pie?** (*pee-eh*)
Stomach?	**¿Estómago?** (*ehs-toh-mah-goh*)
Neck?	**¿Cuello?** (*koo-eh-yoh*)
Eyes?	**¿Ojos?** (*oh-hos*)
Chest?	**¿Pecho?** (*peh-choh*)
Sit here	**Siéntese aquí** (*see-ehn-teh-seh ah-key*)
Lie down here	**Acuéstese aquí** (*ah-kuh-ehs-teh-seh ah-key*)
Don't move.	**No se mueva** (*no seh moo-eh-vah*)
The ambulance is coming	**Viene la ambulancia** (*vee-eh-neh lah ahm-buh-lahn-see-ah*)

Put pressure here	**Ponga presión aquí** (*pohn-gah preh-see-ohn ah-key*)
Do you want to go to a hospital?	**¿Quiere ir al hospital?** (*key-eh--reh eer ahl ohs-pee-tahl*)
Your husband/child/wife is OK.	**Su esposo/esposa/niño está bien** (*suh ehs-poh-so/ehs-poh-sah/ nehn-yo ehs-tah bee-ehn*)

COMMERCIAL VEHICLE INSPECTIONS

I need to see your drivers license

Necesito ver su licencia para manejar (*neh-seh-see-toh vehr soo lee-sehn-see-ah pah-rah mah-neh-har*)

Your license has expired

Su licencia ha expirado (*soo lee-sehn-see-ah ah es-peeh-rrah-doh*)

You do not have the correct type of license

No tiene el tipo corecto de licencia para manejar (*noh tee-eh-neh ehl tee-poh koh-rehk-toh deh lee-sehn-see-ah pah-rah mah-neh-har*)

You committed a traffic infraction

Ha cometido una infracción de tráfico (*ah koh-meh-tee-doh oo-nah ehn-frahk-see-ohn deh trah-fee-koh*)

Do you have vehicle insurance?

¿Tiene seguro del vehículo? (*tee-eh-neh seh-goo-roh dehl veh-ee-koo-loh*)

Do you have a logbook?

¿Tiene la libreta de horario? (*tee-eh-neh lah lee-breh-tah deh oh-rah-ree-oh*)

Do you have a medical certificate?	¿Tiene un certificado médico? (*tee-eh-neh oon sehr-ee-fee-kah-doh meh-dee-koh*)
Vehicle registration?	¿Registro del vehículo? (*reh-hees-troh dehl veh-ee-koo-loh*)
Trailer registration?	¿Registro del remolque? (*reh-hees-troh dehl reh-mohl-keh*)
I need to inspect your load	Nesecito inspeccionar su cargamento (*neh-seh-see-toh eens-pekh-see-oh-nahr soo cahr-gah-mehn-toh*)
I need to see your manifest	Nesecito ver su manifiesto (*neh-seh-see-toh vehr soo mahn-nee-fee-ehs-toh*)
I am going to inspect your tractor	Voy a inspeccionar su tractor (*voh-ee ah eens-pehk-see oh-nahr soo trahk-tohr*)
Start your motor	Prenda el motor (*prehn-dah ehl moh-tohr*)
Apply the brakes	Aplique los frenos (*ah-plee-keh lohs freh-nos*)
Release the brakes	Suelte los frenos (*soo-ehl-teh lohs freh-nos*)
Turn the left turn signal on.	Ponga la direccional izquierda (*pohn-gah lah dee-rehk- see-oh-nahl ees-kee-erh-dah*)

Turn the right turn signal on	**Ponga la direccional derecha** (*pohn-gah lah dee-rehk-see-oh-nahl deh-reh-cha*)
Turn on the headlights	**Encienda las luces delanteras** (*ehn-see-ehn-dah lahs loo-sehs deh-lahn-teh-rahs*)
Turn off the motor	**Apague el motor** (*ah-pah-geh ehl moh-tohr*)
Open the engine compartment	**Abra el compartimiento del motor** (*ah-brah ehl kohm-pahr-tee-mehn-toh dehl moh-tohr*)
You have defective injectors	**Tiene inyectores malos** (*tee-eh-neh een-yehk-toh-rehs mah-lohs*)
The air tank does not work correctly	**El tanque de aire no funciona bien** (*ehl tahn-keh deh ah-ee-reh noh foon-see-oh-nah bee-ehn*)
Your brakes are defective	**Sus frenos están defectuosos** (*soos freh-nohs ehs-stahn- deh-fehk-tuh-oh-sohs*)
Your load is too heavy	**Su cargamento es desmasiado pesado** (*soo kahr-gah- mehn-toh ehs deh-mah-see-ah-doh peh-sah-doh*)
I need to see your emergency equipment.	**Nesecito ver su equipo de emergencia** (*neh-seh-see-toh vehr soo eh-kee-poh deh eh-mehr-hehn-see-ah*)
Fire Extinguisher	**Extinguidor** (*ex-teen-gih-dohr*)

Reflectors	**Reflectores** (*reh-flehk-toh-rehs*)
I am giving you a warning, it is not a citation	**Voy a darle un aviso, no es una multa** (*voh-ee ah dahr-leh oon ah-vee-soh, no ehs uh-nah muhl-tah*)
This vehicle is out of service	**Este vehículo esta fuera de servicio** (*ehs-teh veh-ee-koo-loh ehs-tah foo-ehr-ah deh sehr-vee-see-oh*)
You cannot move this vehicle until it is repaired	**No puede mover este vehículo hasta que sea reparado** (*noh poo-eh-deh moh-ver ehs-teh veh-ee-koo-loh ahs-tah keh say-ah reh-pah-rah-doh*)
Do you have a mechanic?	**¿Tiene un mecánico?** (*tee-eh-neh uhn meh-kah-nee-koh*)
Do you want a tow truck?	**¿Desea una grúa?** (*deh-seh-ah oo-nah groo-ah*)
I am giving you a citation for _____	**Voy a darle una multa por** (*voh-ee ah dahr-leh oo-nah muhl-tah pohr* _____)

Signing this citation is not an admission of guilt	**Firmar la multa no es admitir culpabilidad** (*feer-mahr lah mool-tah noh ehs ahd-mee-teer kool-pah-bee-lee-dahd*)
Only a promise to appear in court	**Sólo una promesa de presentarse en la corte** (*soh-loh oo-nah pro-meh-sah deh preh-sehn-tahr-seh ehn lah kohr-teh*)
Go to this court _____	**Vaya a esta corte** (*vah-yah ah ehs-tah korh-teh*)
At this address_____	**En esta dirección** (*ehn ehs-tah dee-rehk see-ohn*)
In this city_____	**En esta ciudad** (*ehn ehs-tah see-oo-dahd*)
On this date_____	**En esta fecha** (*ehn-ehs-tah feh-chah*)
At this time_____	**A esta hora** (*ah ehs-tah oh-rah*)
Do you understand?	**¿Entiende?** (*ehn-tee-ehn-deh*)
Do you have any questions?	**¿Tiene algunas preguntas?** (*tee-eh-neh ahl-goo-nahs preh-goon-tahs*)

WORDS ASSOCIATED WITH INSPECTIONS

Air Hose	**Manguera de aire** (*mahn-geh-rah deh ah-ee-reh*)
Axle (Front/Rear)	**Eje (Frontero / Trasero)** (*eh-heh (frohn-teh-roh/trah-seh-roh)*)
Battery	**Batería** (*bah-teh-ree-ah*)
Bill of Lading	**Documento de embarque** (*doh-koo-mehn-toh deh ehm-bahr-keh*)
Brake Adjusters	**Adjustadores de freno** (*ah-hoos-tah-doh-rehs deh freh-nohs*)
Brake Shoes	**Barras de frenos** (*bah-rrahs deh freh-nohs*)
Brake Drums	**Tambores de frenos** (*tahm boh-rehs deh freh-nohs*)
Brake Lights	**Luces de frenos** (*loo-sehs deh freh-nohs*)
Bumper	**Parachoques** (*pah-rah-choh-kehs*)
Cargo	**Cargamento** (*kahr-gah-mehn-toh*)
Clutch	**Embrague** (*ehm-brah-geh*)
Daily Inspection Report	**Informe diario de inspección** (*een-forh-meh dee-ah-reh-oh deh eens-pehk-see-ohn*)

Door	**Puerta** (*poo-ehr-tah*)
Driver	**Chofer** (*choh-fehr*)
Electrical System	**Sistema elétrico** (*sees-teh-mah eh-lehk-treh-koh*)
Fan Belt	**Correa de ventilador** (*koh-rreh-ah deh vehn tee-lah-dohr*)
Fan	**Ventilador** (*vehn-tee-lah-dohr*)
Flat Tire	**Llanta desinflada** (*yahn-tah dehs-ihn-flah-dah*)
Frame	**Estructura** (*ehs-trook-too-rah*)
Fuel tank	**Tanque de gasolina** (*tahn-keh deh gah-soh-lee-nah*)
Gear Shift	**Palanca de cambios** (*pah-lahn-kah deh cahm-bee-ohs*)
Haz/Mat Placard	**Aviso de material peligroso** (*ah-veeh-soh deh mah-teh-ree-ahl peh-lee-groh-soh*)
Headlights	**Luces delanteras** (*loo-sehs deh-lahn-teh-rahs*)
Heater	**Calefacción** (*kah-leh-fahk-see-ohn*)
Hood	**Capó** (*kah-poh*)
Ignition	**Arranque** (*ah-rrahn-keh*)
Instruments	**Instrumentos** (*eens-troo-mehn-tohs*)

Leak	**Gotera** (*goh-teh-rah*)
Oil	**Aceite** *(ah-ceh-teeh)*
Fuel (diesel)	**Diesel** *(deeh-sell)*
Hydraulic	**Hidráulico** *(ee-drah-uu-lee-koh)*
License Plate	**Placa** (*plah-kah*)
Motor	**Motor** (*moh-tohr*)
Starting Motor	**Motor de partida** (*moh-tohr deh pahr-tee-dah*)
Steering Wheel	**Volante** (*voh-lahn-teh*)
Tire(s)	**Llanta(s)** (*yahn-tah(s)*)
Tractor	**Tractor** (*track-tohr*)
Trailer	**Remolque** (*reh-mohl-keh*)
Transmission	**Transmisión** (*trahns-mee-see-ohn*)
Truck	**Camión** (*kah-mee-ohn*)
Turn Signal	**Direccional** (*dee-rehk-see-oh-nahl*)
Out-of-service	**Fuera de servicio** (*foo-eh-rah deh sehr-vee-see-oh*)
Wheel	**Rueda** (*roo-eh-dah*)
Windshield Wiper	**Limpiaparabrisas** (*leem-pee-ah-pah-rah-bree-sahs*)

AREA OPEN FOR NOTES:

CHAPTER SIX

Weapons / Danger Phrases &

Drug phrases

In law enforcement, officer safety and survival skills are a key component of everyday strategy. Being aware of your surroundings and what can be used as a weapon against you is worth taking the time to study this section. Granted slang for words always change and meanings could be different depending who is using a word or phrase relating to a weapon. The below list are the most commonly used words:

AK-47.........................**El Cuerno, El Cuerno de Chivo, La Escucharda** *(ehl koo-ehr-noh, ehl koo-ehr-noh deh chee-voh, lah ehs-koo-charh-dah)*

Axe/hatchet....................**La Hacha** *(lah ah-cha)*

Baseball bat...................**El Palo de béisbol** *(ehl pah-loh deh beh-ees-bohl)*

Billiard cue....................**El Taco de Billar** *(ehl tah-koh deh bee-yahr)*

Billy club.......................**La Macana** *(lah mah-cah-nah)*

Bottle...........................**La Botella** *(lah boh-tay-yah)*

Bomb...........................**La Bomba** *(lah bohm-bah)*

Brass knuckles...............**Las Manoplas** *(lahs mah-noh-plahs)*

Brick............................**El Ladrillo** *(ehl lah-dree-yoh)*

Chain...........................**La Cadena** *(lah cah-deh-nah)*

Club............................**El Garrote / El Palo** *(ehl gah-roh-the/ehl pah-loh)*

Dagger........................**El Puñal / La Daga** *(ehl puh-nyal/lah dah-gah)*

Dynamite.....................**La Dinamita** *(lah deh-nah-meeh-tah)*

Explosives...................**Los Explosivos** *(lohs ehs-ploh-see-vohs)*

Firearm.......................**El Cuete / El Hierro (slang)** *(ehl cuh-eh-teh/ehl ee-ehr-roh)*

Hammer......................**El Martillo** *(ehl mahr-tee-yoh)*

Ice Pick.......................**El Picahielo** *(ehl pee-kah yeh-loh)*

Knife...........................**La Navaja / El Cuchillo / El Filero** *(lah nah-vah-hah / ehl koo-che-yoh / ehl fee-leh-rroh)*

Machete......................**El Machete** *(ehl mah-cheh-teh)*

Metal Bar....................**La Barra de Metal** *(lah bah-rrah-deh meh-tahl)*

Needle / Syringe................**La Aguja / Jeringa** *(lah ah-guh-ha)/ (heeh-ring-gah)*

Pipe............................**La Pipa / El Tubo** *(lah pee-pah/ehl too-boh)*

Pistol...........................**La Pistola** *(lah peh-stoh-lah)*

Rifle............................**El Rifle** *(ehl ree-flay)*

Rock/Stone......................**La Roca / La Piedra** *(lah roh-kah/lah pee-eh-drah)*

Rope............................**La Soga** *(lah soh-gah)*

Saw.............................**El Serrucho** *(ehl seh-rooh-choh)*

Scissors........................**Las Tijeras** *(lahs tee-hehr-ahs)*

Screwdriver.....................**El Destornillador** *(ehl dehs-tohr-nee-yah-dohr)*

Semi-automatic.................**La Semiautomática** *(lah seh-mee-ow-toh-mah-tee-kah)*

Shotgun........................**La Escopeta** *(lah ehs-koh-peh-tah)*

Shovel..........................**La Pala** *(lah pah-lah)*

Stick...........................**El Palo** *(ehl pah-loh)*

Sword..........................**La Espada** *(lah ehs-pah-dah)*

Whip...........................**El Látigo** *(ehl lah-tee-goh)*

Wire………………………..**El Alambre** *(ehl ah-lahm-bray)*

Wrench……………………..**La Llave** *(lah yah-veh)*

NOTES:

DANGER PHRASES

In this section, the words contained relating to danger phrases are **_Mexican phraseology_**. These words and phrases are commonly used by Mexican people, however, due to the fact that our world has become transnational within the Spanish speaking world, other Spanish speakers may also utilize these words and phrases.

The following six lines may or may not be a pre-cursor to any of the following words or statements. Pay close attention to ALL words spoken around you. One person may simply say a **_single_** word to another person and that word could mean your demise. Please study this section over and over!

If he/she becomes careless...............**Si se descuida**
(see seh dehs-koo-eh-dah)

When he/she becomes careless..........**Cuando se descuide**
(koo-ahn-doh say dehs- koo-eh-day)

If he/she turns around....................**Si se voltea**
(see seh vohl-teh-ah)

When he/she turns around...............**Cuando se voltee**
(koo-ahn-doh say vohl-teh-eh)

If he/she falls asleep or gets careless...**Si se duerme**
(see say doo-erh-meh)

When he/she goes to sleep
or gets careless..........................**Cuando se duerma**
(koo-ahn-doh say doo-erh-mah)

The following expressions "may" OR "maynot" complete a thought from the above statements.

All fucked up............................	**La verga / Para la verga** *(lah verh-gah / pah-rah lah verh-gah)*
Be alert....................................	**Pónte Trucha** *(pohn-teh truh-chah)*
Be alert....................................	**Pónte Truman** *(pohn-teh truh-mahn)*
Be alert....................................	**Truman** *(truh-mahn)*
Be alert....................................	**Aguas** (literally means waters) *(ah-gu-wahs)*
Be careful/caution......................	**Cuidado** *(koo-ee-dah-doh)*
Beat him/her bad.......................	**Dale en la madre** *(dah-leh ehn lah mah-dreh)*
Cow...	**Vaca** *(vah-kah)*
Dumb.......................................	**Menso/mensa** *(mehn-soh / mehn-sah)*
Dumb.......................................	**Memo/mema** *(meh-moh / meh-mah)*
Fuck all this.............................	**Pa la verga** *(pah lah verh-gah)*
Get ready.................................	**Abusado** *(ah-buh-sah-doh)*
Get ready	**Pónte abusado** *(pohn teh ah-buh-sah-doh)*
Grab her..................................	**Agárrala** *(ah-gah-rrah-lah)*
Grab him.................................	**Agárralo** *(ah-gah-rrah-loh)*
Grab her (fuck her up)................	**Cójela** *(koh-heh-lah)*
Grab him (fuck him up)..............	**Cójelo** *(koh-heh-loh)*
Grab his/her thing (gun).............	**Cójele la cosa** *(koh-heh-leh lah koh-sah)*
Grab his/her thing (gun).............	**Chingale la cosa** *(chihn-gah-leh lah koh-sah)*

Grab his/her gun................................	**Agarrale, la pistola, el cuete, el hierro** *(ah-gah-rrah- leh) (lah peh-stoh-lah, ehl koo-eh-teh, ehl ee-eh-rroh)*
Grab or take away his/her the gun............	**Chíngale la pistol** *(chehn-gah-leh lah pehs-toh-lah)*
Grab or take away his/her gun.................	**Chíngale el cuete** *(chehn-gah-leh ehl koo-eh-teh)*
Grab or take away his/her iron................	**Chíngale el hierro** *(chehn-gah-leh ehl ee-eh-rroh)*
Grab or take away the killer...................	**Chíngale la matona** *(chehn-gah-leh lah mah-tohn-ah)*
Grab or take away the fucking thing..........	**Chíngale la chingadera** *(chehn-gah-leh lah chehn-gah-dehr-ah)*
Grab or take away the thing...................	**Chíngale la cosa** *(chehn-gah-leh lah koh-sah)*
Grab or take away the whatchamacallit.......	**Chíngale la desta** *(chehn-gah-leh lah dehs-tah)*
Here he/she comes.............................	**Ahí Viene** *(ah-ee vee-ehn-eh)*
Here they come................................	**Ahí vienen** *(ah-ee vee-eh-nehn)*
Hit him/her.....................................	**Dale un golpe** *(dah-leh uhn gohl-peh)*
Hit him/her.....................................	**Dale un putazo** *(dah-leh uhn puh-tah-soh)*
Hit him/her.....................................	**Pégale** *(peh-gah-leh)*
Hit him/her.....................................	**Dale un cabronazo** *(dah-leh uhn kah-broh-nah-soh)*

Hit him/her	**Dale un madrazo** *(dah-leh uhn mah-drah-soh)*
Hit him/her	**Dale un chingazo** *(dah-leh uhn chen-gah-soh)*
Idiot	**Idiota** *(ee-dee-oh-tah)*
Jump him/her	**Bríncale** *(breehn-kah-leh)*
Kill her	**Mátala** *(mah-tah-lah)*
Kill her (fuck her)	**Jódela** *(hoh-deh-lah)*
Kill her	**Chíngala** *(chehn-gah-lah)*
Kill him/her	**Dale en la madre** *(dah-leh ehn lah mah-dreh)*
Kill him	**Mátalo** *(mah-tah-loh)*
Kill him	**Chíngalo** *(chehn-gah-loh)*
Kill him (fuck him)	**Jódelo** *(hoh-deh-loh)*
Let's go in a hurry	**Vamanos de chinga** *(vah-mah-nohs deh chen-gah)*
Let's go now. Let's do it now!	**¡Vamanos!** *(vah-mah-nohs)*
Let's get the hell out of here!	**¡Vamos en chinga!** *(vah-mohs ehn chen-gah)*
Look out	**Ojo** *(oh-hoh)*
Nail him	**Clávalo** *(klah-vah-loh)*
Nail her	**Clávala** *(klah-vah-lah)*
New rookie (female)	**Novata/novatona** *(noh-vah-tah / noh-vah-toh-nah)*
New rookie (male)	**Novato/novatón** *(noh-vah-toh / noh-vah-tohn)*
Now	**En chinga** *(ehn chen-gah)*
Now! Do it!	**¡Orale!** *(ohr-ah-leh)*
Ox	**Buey** *(booh-eh)*

Run...	**Córrele** *(koh-rreh-leh)*
Shoot her.....................................	**Cuetéala** *(koo-ee-teh-ah-lah)*
Shoot him....................................	**Cuetéalo** *(koo-ee-teh-ah-loh)*
Stab her......................................	**Clavala** *(klah-vah-lah)*
Stab her......................................	**Navajéala** *(nah- vah-heh-ah-lah)*
Stab him.....................................	**Clavalo** *(klah-vah-loh)*
Stab him.....................................	**Navajéalo** *(nah-vah-heh-ah-loh)*
Stab her......................................	**Filéala** *(fee-leh-ah-lah)*
Stab him.....................................	**Filéalo** *(fee-leh-ah-loh)*
Stick him/her...............................	**Picalo/picala** *(pee-kah-loh / pee-kah-lah)*
He looks very stupid.....................	**Se ve muy pendejo** *(say veh moo-ee pehn-deh-hoh)*
She looks very stupid....................	**Se ve muy pendeja** *(say ve moo-ee pehn-deh-hah)*
He seems very stupid....................	**Parece muy pendejo** *(pah-reh-say moo-ee pehn-deh-hoh)*
She seems very stupid...................	**Parece muy pendeja** *(pah-reh-say moo-ee pehn-deh-hah)*
We'll fuck her (kill her)................	**La jodemos** *(lah hoh-deh-mohs)*
We'll fuck him (kill him)..............	**Lo jodemos** *(loh-hoh-deh-mohs)*
We'll grab her..............................	**La agarramos** *(lah ah-gah-rrah-mohs)*
We'll grab him.............................	**Lo agarramos** *(loh ah-gah-rrah-mohs)*
We'll grab her (fuck her)..............	**La cogemos** *(lah koh-heh-mohs)*

We'll grab him (fuck him)..................**Lo cogemos** *(loh koh-heh-mohs)*
We'll hit him/her............................**Le pegamos** *(leh peh-gah-mohs)*
We'll jump him/her,,,,,,,,,,,,,,,,,, **Le brincamos** *(leh brehn-kah-mohs)*

*Concerning Mexican Spanish - there are three verbs that are frequently used to indicate the English translation of: To Fuck. These verbs are: **Chingar**, **Cojer** and **Joder**. The information provided above is vulgar language used mostly by Mexicans. Mexicans are not the only persons who utilize vulgar words, however, this section relates to Mexican slang. Translations of these three verbs may change in other Spanish speaking countries.

DRUGS AND DRUG PHRASEOLOGY

Any law enforcement officer knows that drugs are a menace to our cultural society. Albeit prescription drugs or illegal drugs, the likelihood of encountering drugs on a daily basis is commonplace.

The below section is provided with the most common known narcotics, legal or illegal, The slang words associated to these drugs often change regionally and by country. I have tried my best to give to you the most up to date of drug terms. Just because the word sounds like it does not mean a drug, drug users commonly change the meanings to commonly used words.

Brown heroin............	**heroína marron** *(ehr-oh-eeh-nah mah-rrohn)*, **el fango** *(ehl fahn-goh)*
Cocaine....................	**cocaina** *(koh-kah-eeh-nah)*, **la coca** *(lah koh-kah)*, **la ñieve** *(lah neeh-eh-veh)*, **el polvo** *(ehl pohl-voh)*, **la mujer blanca** *(lah muh-hehr blahn-kah)*, **el perico** *(ehl pehr-eeh-koh)*, **un popon** *(uhn poh-pohn)*, **un siete** *(uhn see-eh-teh)*, **una onza** *(ooh-nah ohn-sah)*
Crack.......................	**el crack** *(ehl krahk)*, **una piedra** *(uh-nah peeh-eh-drah)*
Fentanyl...................	**fentanilo** *(fehn-tah-neeh-loh)*, **la ese** *(lah eh-say)*
Hashish....................	**el chocolate** *(ehl choh-koh-lah-teh)*, **el hachi** *(ehl ah-chey)*, **la grifa** *(lah greh-fah)*, **el kif** *(ehl keef)*
Heroin.....................	**el hero** *(ehl eh-roh)*, **la manteca** *(lah mahn-teh-kah)*, **la chiva** *(lah chee-vah)*, **el caballo** *(ehl kah-bah-yoh)*, **el caballo blanco** *(ehl kah-bah-yoh blahn-koh)*, **heroína** *(hehr-oh-eehn-nah)*, **carga** *(kahr-gah)*, **de la negra** *(deh lah neh-grah)*

Joints........................los leños *(lohs leh-neeh-yos)*, el pito *(ehl peeh-toh)*, un toque *(uhn toh-kahy)*
LSD.........................el acido *(ehl aah-see-doh)*, el sello *(ehl say-yoh)*, el pegao *(ehl pay-gah-oh)*
Marijuana..................la yerba *(lah yehr-bah)*, la mota *(lah moh-tah)* or el moto *(ehl moh-toh)*, el zacate *(ehl sah-kah-teh)*, el pasto *(ehl pahs-toh)*, yucatan *(yuuh-kah-than)*, zorrillo *(soh-rreh-oh)*, la grifa *(lah greeh-fah)*, de la verde *(deh lah vehr-deh)*
Mescaline...................mescalina *(mehs-kah-leeh-nah)*
MDMA(Ecstacy)..........equis *(eeh-keeys)*, penguas *(pehn-gooh-ahs)*
Meth........................metadina *(meh-tah-deehn-ah)*, ventana *(vehn-tahn-ah)*, vidrio *(veeh-dreeh-oh)*, helondo *(eeh-lohn-doh)*, cristal *(kreehs-tahl)*
Opium.......................opio *(ooh-pee-oh)*
Oxycodone..................oxicodona *(ohx-eeh-koh-dohn-ah)*
PCP (angel dust)........... el polvo de angel *(ehl pohl-voh deh ahn-hehl)*
Peyote.......................peyote *(pay-yoh-teh)*
Psychodelic Mushrooms...setas psicodélico *(seeh-tahs seeh-koh-dehl-eeh-koh)*, shrooms *(shroohms)*
Roach........................la cucaracha *(lah koo-kah-rah-chah)*, la chicharra *(lah cheh-charh-rah)*, un toque *(uhn tooh-kay)*

Slang Terminolgy

Snow	la ñieve
Female goat	la chiva
Powder	el polvo
Weed	la yerba, hierba
Grass/hay	el zacate
Brown mud	el fango
Acid	el acido
Seal, stamp	el sello
Sticky	el pegao
Pieces of wood	los leños
Whistle	el pito
Lard	la manteca
Horse	el caballo
My thing "drugs/stash/money, etc"	mi jale
Money	dinero, peso, pisto, lana, feria

AREA OPEN FOR NOTES:

AREA OPEN FOR NOTES:

Below you will find some basic questions to begin a dialog with a person with whom you have made contact with relating to narcotics. Granted there are a million questions that can be asked relating to this topic, however, I have provided some beginning questions to open a conversation.

Initial Contact Questions Relating to Narcotics

Do you sell drugs?
¿Vende usted las drogas?
(¿vehn-deh oo-stehd lahs droh-gahs?)

Do you know anyone who sells drugs?
¿Conoce a alguien que vende las drogas?
(¿koh-noh-say ah ahl-gee-ehn keh vehn-deh lahs droh-gahs?)

Have you heard of anyone selling drugs?
¿Ha oído a alguien que vende las drogas?
(¿ah oh-eeh-doh ah ahl-gee-ehn keh vehn-deh lahs droh-gahs?)

Where are they from? What country?
¿De dónde son? ¿Qué país?
(¿day dohn-deh sohn? ¿keh pah-ees?)

Transportation / Concealment / Storage Areas

What persons or groups are involved?
¿Qué personas o grupos están involucrados?
(¿keh perh-soh-nahs oh gruh-pohs ehs-tahn en-vo-luh-crah-dohs?)

Are they involved in a drug cartel?
¿Están involucrados en un cártel de drogas?
(¿ehs-tahn en-vo-luh-crah-dos ehn uhn karh-tehl deh droh-gahs?)

What is the name of the cartel?
¿Cuál es el nombre del cartel?
(¿koo-ahl ehs ehl nohm-breh dehl kahr-tehl?)

What buildings or cars are used?
¿Qué edificios o carros se utilizan?
(¿keh eh-dee-fee-see-ohs oh kahr-ohs say oo-tee-lee-sahn?)

What arrangements are made to move, to buy and to sell drugs?
¿Qué arreglos están hechos para moverse, para comprar y vender a las drogas?
(¿keh ah-rreh-glohs ehs-tahn eh-chohs pah-rah moh-verh-say, pah-rah kohm-prahr ee vehn-dehr ah lahs droh-gahs?)

How many people move the drugs?
¿Cuántas personas se mueven las drogas?
(¿kuh-ahn-tohs pehr-sohn-ahs say muh-eh-vehn lahs droh-gahs?)

Who are they? Their names.
¿Quiénes son? Sus nombres.
(¿key-ehn-ehs sohn? suhs nohm-brehs.)

Do you know the routes?
¿Conoce las rutas?
(¿koh-noh-say lahs ruh-tahs?)

Do they use the same routes?
> **¿Se usan las mismas rutas?**
> *(¿say uh-sahn lahs mehs-mahs ruh-tahs?)*

Obtaining and Moving Drugs

How is contact made for drug orders?
> **¿Cómo se puso en contacto para los pedidos de las drogas?**
> *(¿koh-moh say puh-soh ehn kohn-tahk-toh pah-rah lohs peh-dee-dohs day lahs droh-gahs?)*

Who obtains the drugs, transports the drugs and maintains security for the drugs?
> **¿Quién obtiene las drogas, transporta y mantenga la seguridad de las drogas?**
> *(¿key-ehn ohb-tee-ehn-ee lahs droh-gahs. trahns-porh-tah ee mahn-tehn-gah lah say-guhr-ee-dahd day lahs droh-gahs?)*

How do you communicate with each other while transporting the drugs?
> **¿Cómo se comunica, mientras que el transporte de las drogas?**
> *(¿koh-moh say koh-muhn-ee-kah, mee-ehn-trahs keh ehl trahns-porh-teh deh lahs droh-gahs?)*

BUILDINGS / OFFICES & CONTENTS

airport..........................**el aeropuerto** *(ehl ah-roh-pooh-ahr toh)*

apartment(s)....................**el/los apartamento(s)** *(ehl / lohs ah-pahr-tah-mehn-toh (tohs))*

chair............................**la silla** *(lah see-yah)*

bakery..........................**la panadería** *(lah pah-nah-deh-ree-yah)*

bank............................**el banco** *(ehl bahn-koh)*

bar.............................**el bar or la cantina** *(ehl bahr or lah kahn-tee-nah)*

barber shop.....................**la peluquería** *(lah pee-luh-kay-ree-ah)*

beauty salón....................**el salón de belleza** *(ehl sah-lohn day beeh-yeh-sah)*

book store......................**la librería** *(lah lee-breh-reeh-ah)*

bus station.....................**la estación de autobús** *(lah ehs-tah-see-ohn day ah-ooh-toh-boohs)*

business........................**el negocio** *(ehl neh-goh-see-oh)*

church..........................**la iglesia** *(lah eeh-gleh-see-ah)*

clinic..........................**la clínica** *(lah klihn-eeh-kah)*

146

college............................**el colegio** *(ehl kooh-leeh-he-oh)*

courthouse.......................**el palacio de justicia** *(ehl pah-lah-see-oh day hoohs-tee-see-ah)*

desk..............................**el escritorio** *(ehl ehs-creeh-tohr-eeh-oh)*

elevator.........................**el elevador** *(ehl ehl-eh-vah-dohr)*

entrance........................**la entrada** *(lah ehn-trah-dah)*

escalator........................**la escalera mecánica** *(lah ehs-kah-lehr-ah may-kahn-eeh-kah)*

exit...............................**la salida** *(lah sah-leeh-dah)*

factory..........................**la fábrica** *(lah fah-breeh-kah)*

fire department.................**el departamento de bomberos** *(ehl day-pahr-tah-mehn-toh day bohm-behr-ohs)*

fire escape......................**la salida de emergencia** *(lah sah-leeh-dah day eh-mehr-hehn-see-ah)*

floor (stand on).................**el piso / el suelo** *(ehl peeh-soh / ehl suh-eh-loh)*

florist............................**la floristería** *(lah flohr-eehs-tehr-eeh-ah)*

furniture store..................**la mueblería** *(lah mooh-ehb-lehr-eeh-ah)* gas station......................**la gasolinera** *(lah gah-soh-leeh-nehr-ah)*

grocery store....................**el mercado or la bodega** *(ehl mehr-kah-doh or lah boh-deh gah)*

ground..........................**el suelo** *(ehl suh-eh-loh)*

hospital.........................**el hospital** *(ehl ohs-peeh-tahl)*

jail..............................**el cárcel** *(ehl kahr-cehl)*

jewelry store...................**la joyería** *(lah hoy-ehr-eeh-ah)*

laundromat....................**la lavandería** *(lah lah-vahn-deeh-reh-ah)*

library..........................**la biblioteca** *(lah beeh-bleeh-oh-teeh-kah)*

level (story)....................**el nivel** *(ehl neeh-vehl)*

light (as in bulb)...............**la luz** *(lah luuhs)*

lobby...........................**el salón** *(ehl sah-lohn)*

key(s)..........................**la/las llave(s)** *lah / lahs yah-veeh (veehs))*

meat market....................**la carnicería** *(lah kahr-neeh-cehr-eeh-ah)*

movies (theater)................**el cine** *(ehl see-nahy)*

museum........................**el museo** *(ehl mooh-say-oh)*

office.............................	**la oficina** *(lah oh-feeh-see-nah)*
pawn shop.......................	**la casa de empeño** *(lah kah-sah day ehm-pahy-nee-oh)*
pharmacy........................	**la farmacia** *(lah fahr-mah-see-ah)*
police station...................	**el estación de policía** *(ehl ehs-tah-see-ohn day poh-lee-see-ah)*
pool hall.........................	**la sala de biliar** *(lah sah-lah day beeh-leeh-ahr)*
post office.......................	**la oficina de correos** *(lah ooh-feeh-see-nah day koh-rreeh-ohs)*
repair shop(auto)..............	**el taller mecánico** *(ehl tah-yehr mahy-kahn-eeh-koh)*
restaurant.......................	**el restaurante** *(ehl rehs-tah-ooh-rahn-tahy)*
restroom.........................	**el baño** *(ehl bah-nyoh)*
school.............................	**la escuela** *(lah ehs-kooh-ehl-ah)*
elementary school............	**la escuela primaria** *(lah ehs-kooh-ehl-ah preeh-mahr-eeh-ah)*
high school......................	**el colegio** *(ehl kooh-leh-heeh-oh)*
university.......................	**la universidad** *(lah uhn-neeh-vehr-see-dahd)*

shoe store.......................**la zapatería** *(lah sah-pah-tehr-eeh-ah)*

stairway.........................**área de escaleras** *(ah-reeh-ah day ehs-kah-lehr-ahs)*

store............................**la tienda** *(lah teeh-ehn-dah)*

supermarket.....................**el supermercado** *(ehl sooh-pehr-mehr-kah-doh)*

table..............................**la mesa** *(lah mahy-sah)*

warehouse.......................**el almacén** *(ehl ahl-mah-seen)*

THE HOUSE

attic............................**el ático or el desván** *(ehl ah-teeh-koh or ehl dehs-vahn)*

basement.......................**el sotano** *(ehl sooh-tah-noh)*

bathroom.......................**el baño** *(ehl bah-nyoh)*

bathroom sink..................**el lava manos** *(ehl lah-vah mah-nohs)*

bed.............................**la cama** *(lah kah-mah)*

bedroom........................**la recámara** *(lah rahy-kah-mah-rrah)*

bookcase.......................**el estante** *(ehl ehs-tahn-tahy)*

carpet..........................**el tapete** *(ehl tah-pahy-teh)*

chair	**la silla** *(lah see-yah)*
ceiling	**el techo** *(ehl teeh-choh)*
curtains	**las cortinas** *(lahs kohr-teeh-nahs)*
dining room	**el comedor** *(ehl koh-mah-dohr)*
door	**la puerta** *(lah-pooh-ehr-tah)*
dresser	**el tocador** *(ehl toh-kah-dohr)*
fence	**la cerca** *(lah sehr-kah)*
fireplace	**la chimenea** *(lah chihm-eeh-nahy-ah)*
garage	**el garaje** *(ehl gah-rah-hahy)*
hallway	**el pasillo** *(ehl pah-see-yoh)*
house	**la casa** *(lah kah-sah)*
kitchen	**la cocina** *(lah koh-see-nah)*
kitchen sink	**el lava platos** *(ehl lah-vah plah-tohs)*
lamp	**la lámpara** *(lah lahm-pah-rah)*
living room	**la sala** *(lah sah-lah)*
picture	**el cuadro** *(ehl kooh-ah-droh)*

refrigerator.......................**el refrigerador / la nevera** *(ehl reeh-frih-hehr-ah-dohr / lah neeh-verh-ah)*

room.............................**el cuarto** *(ehl kooh-ahr-toh)*

rug................................**la alfombra** *(lah ahl-foohm-brah)*

telephone........................**el teléfono** *(ehl tahy-leh- fooh-noh)*

toilet.............................**el excusado** *(ehl ehs-kooh-sah-doh)*

sofa..............................**el sofá** *(lah soh-fah)*

stove.............................**la estufa** *(lah ehs-tooh-fah)*

televisión.......................**el televisor** *(ehl teh-leeh-vihs-ohr)*

urinal............................**el inodoro** *(ehl ehn-oh-doh-roh)*

wall..............................**la pared** *(lah pah-rehd)*

window.........................**la ventana** *(lah-vehn-tah-nah)*

HISPANIC CULTURE

DEFINITIONS AND CULTURAL CONSIDERATIONS

UNDERSTANDING HISPANIC NAME COMPOSITION

ORIGINS

The word "**Mexico**" is derived from Mexica (pronounced "Me-shee-ka"), the name for the indigenous group that settled in central Mexico in the early fourteenth century and is best known as the Aztecs.

Red, white, and green are the colors of the national liberation army in Mexico. A ribbon in the national colors is at the bottom of the coat of arms. Throughout history, the flag has changed several times, as the design of the coat of arms and the length-width ratios of the flag have been modified. However, the coat of arms has had the same features throughout: an eagle, holding a serpent in its talon, is perched on top of a prickly pear cactus; the cactus is situated on a rock that rises above a lake. The coat of arms is derived from an Aztec legend that their gods told them to build a city where they spot an eagle on a Nopal eating a serpent, which is now Mexico City.

With a population of 129.2 million as of 2017, Mexico is the ***most populous*** Spanish-speaking country in the world, the second-most populous country in Latin America after Portuguese-speaking Brazil, and the second in North America, after the United States. There are more Spanish speakers in the world than English speakers.

WHAT DOES "HISPANIC" MEAN?

Where did the term "Hispanic" originate within the U.S.? Before 1970, the United States Census Bureau classified Mexican, Cuban and Puerto Rican immigrants as whites. Activists began lobbying the US Census Bureau to create a broad, national category. The result was the creation of the term "Hispanic," first introduced in the US Census in 1970.

POVERTY IN MEXICO

- Around *half* of the population lives in poverty; about 10 percent of people live in *extreme poverty*.
- The number of people in poverty has mainly been increasing since 2012, when 42.9 percent of people were below the national poverty line.
- Chiapas, Guerrero and Puebla are the states with the highest levels of poverty..
- There are 31 states in Mexico as well as one Federal District.
- There are no counties or parishes.
- There are no Sheriffs.
- Law enforcement in Mexico is divided between federal, state, and municipal entities.
- As of 2012, Mexico has a police force of over 544,000 people, making it the country with the fourth largest police force in the world.

MEXICAN HOLIDAYS AND CELEBRATIONS

- In Mexico there are 3 major kinds of holidays and celebrations:

- **Statutory Holiday:** Holidays observed nationwide and employees (private and public) are entitled to a day off with regular pay.

- **Civic Holiday:** These holidays are observed nationwide, but employees are not entitled to a day-off.

- **Festivities:** These are traditional holidays to honor religious events, such as Carnival, Holy Week, Easter, etc. or public celebrations such as Mother's Day, Father's Day, Valentine's Day, etc.

5th of May Cinco de Mayo	Celebrates the victory of the Mexican Army, led by Gen. Ignacio Zaragoza, against French forces in the city of Puebla, on May 5, 1862. Also widely celebrated in the United States. US "celebration" of this Mexican historical event is largely a result of promotions in the US by liquor, beer, and bars/taverns/clubs/restaurants since the 1980s. For many years Cinco de Mayo celebrations in the US promoted Cinco de Mayo as Mexican Independence Day which is actually September 16. Although Mexican citizens feel very proud of the meaning of Cinco de Mayo it is not a national holiday in Mexico, but is an official holiday in the State of Puebla where the battle took place.

September 16	**Independence Day**	**Día de Independencia**	Commemorates the start of the Independence War by Father Miguel Hidalgo y Costilla in 1810. This Mexican holiday is similar to the U.S. holiday 4th of July.

NOTES:

OPULENT CELEBRATIONS

Quinceañera

For Hispanic girls in Mexico, Puerto Rico, Cuba, the United States and elsewhere, the 15th birthday marks the most lavish celebration of their lives. Designating a girl's transition from childhood to adulthood, the quinceañera is a two-part festivity that traces back to both indigenous and European cultural traditions and has become an increasingly opulent affair.

> ### Day of the Dead

Dia de los Muertos is celebrated across Mexico, with each region stamping its own cultural mark on the observance. On All Saints Day, Nov. 1, small children who have died are honored as "**angelitos**," little angels. The next day, All Souls Day, is the day set aside for remembering older family members, friends, even the famous who have passed away.

> ### Dia de Nuestra Senora de Guadalupe

She is the patron saint of Mexico, Our Lady of Guadalupe, the dark-skinned Virgin Mary who appeared to Juan Diego, a poor Indian convert to Catholicism, on a hillside near Mexico City in 1531.

RELIGIOUS CELEBRATIONS

Below, you will find a brief list of some of the main celebrations of Mexicans. There are many more and I would encourage you to conduct some research on your own to learn more, not only about Mexicans but other countries of the people you encounter.

> **The Christmas Season**

The Christmas season begins on Dec. 12 and on Dec. 16 children are involved in **Las Posadas**, whereby children, portraying the Holy Family arriving in Bethlehem, go from door to door in the neighborhood seeking shelter. Traditionally, Mexican children received their presents on **Dia de los Santos Reyes**, Three Kings Day. **Lent and Easter**

Mexico celebrates **Carnaval**--Mardi Gras in the U.S.--with raucous parades and displays of conviviality, particularly in Veracruz and Mazatlan, where two of the biggest pre-Lenten celebrations are held. (Dates vary since the fiesta is linked to the Easter calendar.) Mexicans also celebrate **Semana Santa**, Holy Week, with festivals and religious parades on Good Friday and Easter Sunday.

Mexican Baptism

The Catholic religious ceremony is the most important aspect of *el Bautismo*. The child wears a white baptismal garment called a **ropon**; the white color symbolizes purity in the newly baptized. The baptismal candle symbolizes that the child is now enlightened by Christ. Parents choose the godparents of the child very thoughtfully.

HIERARCHY WITHIN A LATINO FAMILY

Father

The father occupies a position of respect and authority. The traditional view of manhood is strongly influenced by *Machismo* - defined as the belief that men should be strong, brave and honorable; they should also protect and provide for their families.

Mother

Mothers in Hispanic culture are the caregivers. Motherhood is highly valued, and families expect women to care for children as well as elderly family members. *Marianismo* is the female version of machismo. Marianismo is the belief that women should be religious, giving and attentive to the needs of their household.

Children

Hispanic families raise children with certain expectations. Parents expect them to be responsible and cooperative and teach them not to talk too much to authority figures and to exhibit emotional restraint. Families expect children to consider the needs of the group and to value interpersonal relationships.

Extended Family

Familyism, the concept of family, is central in the Hispanic community and extends beyond the nuclear family to include grandparents, aunts, uncles and cousins; friends and neighbors; and organizations that are important to the community, such as churches.

MEANING OF TWO SURNAMES IN THE HISPANIC CULTURE

Now, let's look at what is involved in the make-up of a typical "Hispanic" name. The first name is the given name, as in Pablo, Esteban, and Carlos and so on. The next name (the first surname) is the father's surname. The next surname to the right of the first surname is the mother's father's surname, or the mother's maiden name. In the Hispanic culture, the male lineage is the dominant blood line.

GIVEN	FATHER SURNAME	MOTHER SURNAME
JUAN	GOMEZ	SANCHEZ

JUAN: First name, the same as in English speaking countries.

GOMEZ: The family surname of his/her father's bloodline which descends continuously down the male line.

SANCHEZ: The female surname (mother's maiden name as in English speaking countries) for her father's bloodline.

Now, let's look at what happens when there is a marriage. In this example, Juan Gomez Sanchez will marry Maria Cruz Gomez. Pay close attention to the full name of Maria. Her given name is Maria, her father's last name is Cruz and her mother's last name is her father's surname. The male lineage continues even with a female.

GIVEN	**FATHER**	**MOTHER**
JUAN	GOMEZ	SANCHEZ

MARRIES

MARIA	CRUZ	LOPEZ

<u>Maria's new married name will change to:</u>

MARIA	CRUZ	(DE)	GOMEZ

Maria will drop her mother's father's name and take on her new husband's father's name. The word "de" mean "of." In the Hispanic culture it is not uncommon for a last name to have the preposition "of" or in Spanish "de" meaning that she is now of the new family. In this example, Maria is of the Gomez family now.

In my law enforcement career I have seen the following ways in that Mexicans can identify themselfs albeit through a driver's license, government issued form of identification or by word of mouth. Let's take the name of Juan Gomez Sanchez.

In Mexico, he can be leagally identidied as:

Juan Gomez Sanchez
Juan Gomez
Juan Sanchez
Juan G. Sanchez
Juan Gomez S.

So, how in the world can you run this person through NCIC? Not easy to say the very least. You will need to run him in ALL variations of the name. Since our NCIC is not set up to run two last names especially when there is no middle name, you will need to run this person in a combination of names. There is no real easy way to run someone in our current system.

Now let's look at some very familiar names given in the Hispanic culture. There are many names in Spanish that have an English counterpart. Moreover, many names given in Spanish speaking countries have a Biblical foundation:

Spanish	**English**
Samuel	Samuel
Daniel	Daniel
Mateo	Matthew
Marcos	Mark
Lucas	Luke
Juan	John

Joel	Joel
Timoteo	Timothy
Jaime	James
Pedro	Peter
Maria	Mary
José	Joseph
Jesús	Jesus

There are also compound first names given, again representing a Biblical founding:

Male: **José Maria – Joseph Mary**
Female: **Maria José – Mary Joseph**

Additionally, many first names and surnames in the Hispanic culture may also a Biblical meaning:

Cruz – Cross

DelaCruz – Of the Cross

Esperanza – Hope

Gloria – Glory

Rey – King

Reyes – Kings

FAMILY NAMES

In the following section, the names associated within a family are identified. It is very important in knowing these titles within a household. Working knowledge of these names will better assist you when you go to a home for an interview or in conducting community oriented policing. These words will help you personalize your contact with a Hispanic family.

The husband............................	**El marido (esposo)** (*ehl mah-ree-doh /ehs-poh-soh*)
The wife.................................	**La mujer (esposa)** (*lah moo-hehr / ehs-poh-sah*)
The married couple....................	**Los esposos** (*lohs ehs-poh-sohs*)
The grandfather........................	**El abuelo** (*ehl ah-boo-eh-loh*)
The grandmother.......................	**La abuela** (*lah ah-boo-eh-lah*)
The grandparents.......................	**Los abuelos** (*lohs ah-boo-eh-lohs*)
The father................................	**El padre** (*ehl pah-dreh*)
The mother..............................	**La madre** (*lah mah-dreh*)
The parents..............................	**Los padres** (*lohs pah-drehs*)
The son...................................	**El hijo** (*ehl ee-hoh*)
The daughter............................	**La hija** (*lah ee-hah*)

The children............................**Los niños** (*lohs nee-nyos*)

The brother.............................**El hermano** (*ehl ehr-mah-noh*)

The sister,,,,,,,,,,,,,,,...............**La hermana** (*lah ehr-muh-nah*)

The uncle...............................**El tío** (*ehl tee-oh*)

The aunt................................**La tía** (*lah tee-ah*)

The nephew..............................**El sobrino** (*ehl soh-bree-noh*)

The niece...............................**La sobrina** (*lah soh-bree-nah*)

The cousin (male).......................**El primo** (*ehl pree-moh*)

The cousin (female).....................**La prima** (*lah pre-mah*)

The twins...............................**Los mellizos (gemelos)** (*lohs meh-yee-sohs/ heh-meh-lohs*)

The grandson............................**El nieto** (*ehl nee-eh-toh*)

The granddaughter.......................**La nieta** (*lah nee-eh-tah*)

The grandchildren.......................**Los nietos** (*lohs nee-eh-tohs*)

The great grandson......................**El bisnieto** (*ehl bees-nee-eh-toh*)

The great granddaughter.................**La bisnieta** (*lah bees-nee-eh-tah*)

The great grandchildren.................**Los bisnietos** (*lohs bees-nee-eh-tohs*)

The brother-in-law......................**El cuñado** (*ehl koo-nya- doh*)

The sister-in-law……………………**La cuñada** (*lah koo-nya-dah*)

The son-in-law……………………**El yerno** (*ehl yehr-noh*)

The daughter-in-law………………..**La nuera** (*lah noo-eh-rah*)

The father-in-law……………………**El suegro** (*ehl soo-eh-groh*)

The mother-in-law…………………..**La suegra** (*lah soo-eh-grah*)

The stepfather……………………**El padrastro** (*ehl pah-drahs-troh*)

The stepmother…………………..**La madrastra** (*lah mah-drahs-trah*)

The godfather……………………**El padrino** (*ehl pah-dree-noh*)

The godmother…………………..**La madrina** (*lah mah-dree-nah*)

The godparents…………………..**Los padrinos** (*lohs pah-dree-nohs*)

The relatives……………………..**Los parientes** (*lohs pah-ree-ehn-tehs*)

Below, we will tackle what a family tree will look like within a typical Hispanic family. At the top will be the patriarch and matriarch of the family, Carlos and Dora. Below them, there will be the two children of Carlos and Dora, Esteban and Carmen. Esteban will marry Linda Valenzuela de Gomez. Carmen will marry Jesús Martinez Ruiz. Notice how the last names change after marriage of the two females, Linda and Carmen.

Esteban and Linda will have three children, Melinda, Juan and Maria. Carmen and Jesús will have two children, Juanita and José Maria.

Now, following the family tree will be a series of thirteen fill in the blank questions. Look at the family tree, go back to the names of the family members just shown and fill in the blanks, using the correct Spanish word for the family members. Let's see how you do.

NOTES:

CARLOS GOMEZ PRIETA
DORA JUÁREZ GOMEZ

ESTEBAN GOMEZ JUAREZ

MARRIES

LINDA VALENZUELA de GOMEZ

↓

LINDA VALENZUELA de GOMEZ

↓

MELINDA GOMEZ VALENZUELA

JUAN GOMEZ VALENZUELA

MARIA GOMEZ VALENZUELA

CARMEN GOMEZ JUÁREZ

MARRIES

JESÚS MARTINEZ RUIZ

↓

CARMEN GOMEZ de MARTINEZ

↓

JUANITA MARTINEZ GOMEZ

JOSÉ MARIA MARTINEZ GOMEZ

Notice on the left, before Linda marries Esteban, her unmarried name was Linda Valenzuela de Gomez. After she marries Esteban, her now married name is, Linda Valenzuela de Gomez, nothing changes concerning her name. You might be asking how this can be, I'll help answer this. Imagine Carol Smith marries Robert Smith, she is still a Smith, even though she is married. Carol's surname prior to marriage was Smith, then after marriage, she becomes a Smith from a different family, the same applies to Linda as shown above.

La Familía de Melinda

1. Dora es la _____ de Melinda, Juan y Maria.

2. Juan es el _____ de Linda y Esteban.

3. Esteban es el _____ de Linda.

4. Carmen es la _____ de los señores Gomez.

5. Esteban es el _____ de Melinda, Juan y Maria.

6. Carmen es la _____ de Esteban.

7. Juan es el _____ de Carlos y Dora.

8. Linda es la _____ de Melinda, Juan y Maria.

9. Melinda es la _____ de José Maria y Juanita.

10. Linda es la _____ de Esteban.

11. José Maria es el _____ de Melinda, Juan y Maria.

12. Juan es el _____ de Melinda y Maria.

13. Carlos y Dora son los _____ de Melinda, Juan y Maria

Answer the above questions without looking at this answer block.

ANSWERS:

1.abuela	8.madre
2.hijo	9.prima
3.esposo	10.esposa
4.hija	11.primo
5.padre	12.hermano
6.hermana	13.abuelos
7.nieto	

CHAPTER SEVEN

PERCEPTION OF LAW ENFORCEMENT AND NATIONALITIES

The overall perception of law enforcement by Spanish speaking people, in particular Mexican people, is a challenge to all police officers. In Mexico, there are still two main classes of people, those who have and those who have not – the rich and the class that still struggles from day to day. Mexico is still a third world country. Understandably, the poor are making great strides to better themselves. However, poor education and remoteness of many people make the advancement to a better life nearly out of reach for so many.

In Mexico, there is no true NCIC as law enforcement utilizes in the United States. Moreover, with different agencies like the Federal Police, Judicial Police, State Police and Municipal Police, what one law enforcement agency may be doing can be unknown to another agency. The sharing of information, as one can imagine, inevitably is limited or non-existent. The Mexican government has in recent years made inroads to helping the people of Mexico. However, corruption and poor training within law enforcement agencies inhibits proactive police work.

There is a real fear and distrust of many law enforcement officials in Mexico. In Spanish, the word for "bribe" or "being on the take" is *"la mordida"* or *"el mordido."* If you were to travel to Mexico or any other country for that matter, poor pay for law enforcement, remoteness and corruption all play into what many have identified as law enforcement corruption. I am not saying all law enforcement officers in Mexico are on the take, there are many good honest officers, but the pressure is so great, that cracks our law enforcement shell.

Moreover, drug cartels have a near limitless amount of money and resources, facilitating the ability to corrupt law enforcement in Mexico and many other countries. There is a narco term used, *"Plata o Plomo"* "Silver or Lead," take our money or take our lead. Simply put – work for us or we will kill you or someone close to you."

I encourage you to befriend Spanish-speaking families who live in your beat. Show Mexicans and other Spanish speaking people who live or work in your beat respect. What better way to enable them to be an active part of our great country. I can assure you of this, once they can trust you, they will effectively become your eyes and ears in the community they live and you patrol in, a win/win for everyone.

Nationalities

Nationalities are often used troughout investigations. The following words can be useful as you continue your daily work.

Nationalities:

American	**americano** *(ah-mehr-ee-kah-noh)*
Argentinean	**argentino** *(arh-hehn-tee-noh)*
Black	**negro** *(neh-groh)*
Bolivian	**boliviano** *(boh-lee-vee-ah-noh)*
British	**británico** *(breh-tahn-ee-koh)*
Chinese	**chino** *(chee-noh)*
Colombian	**colombiano** *(koo-lohm-bee-ah-noh)*
Cuban	**cubano** *(koo-bahn-oh)*
Dominican (Dominican republic)	**dominicano** *(doh-mehn-ee-kah-noh)*

Ecuadorian	**ecuatoriano** *(eh-koo-ah-torh-ee-ah-noh))*
French	**francés** *(frahn-cehs)*
From the United States	**estadounidense** *(ehs-tah-doh-oo-neh-dehn-say)*
German	**alemán** *(ah-lay-mahn)*
Indian	**indio** *(ehn-dee-oh)*
Iranian	**iraní** *(ee-rahn-ee)*
Iraqi	**iraquí** *(ee-rrah-key)*
Italian	**italiano** *(ee-tah-lee-ah-noh)*
Japanese	**japonés** *(hah-pohn-ehs)*
Korean	**coreano** *(korh-ee-ah-noh)*
Mexican	**mexicano** *(meh-heh-kah-noh)*
North American	**norte americano** *(nohr-teh ah-mehr-ee-kah-noh)*
Oriental	**oriental** *(ohr-ee-ehn-tahl)*
Panamanian	**panameño** *(pah-nah-mehn-yoh)*
Paraguayan	**paraguayo** *(pah-rah-guu-ehy-yoh)*
Peruvian	**peruano** *(perh-uh-ah-noh)*
Polish	**polaco** *(poh-lah-koh)*
Portuguese	**portugués** *(porh-tuh-gehs)*
Puerto Rican	**puertorriqueño** *(poo-ehr-toh-rreh-kane-yoh)*
Russian	**ruso** *(ruh-soh)*
Salvadorian	**salvadoreño** *(salh-vah-dorh-ee-nee-yoh)*
Spanish	**español** *(ehs-pahn-nyol)*
Venezuelan	**venezolano** *(vehn-ee-zoh-lah-noh)*
Vietnamese	**vietnamés** *(vee-eht-nah-mehs)*
White	**blanco** *(blahn-koh)*

CHAPTER EIGHT

ASKING AND ANSWERING QUESTIONS

MIRANDA WARNING

ASSAULT / DOMESTIC VIOLENCE

SEXUAL ASSUALT / HOMICIDE INVESTIGATIONS

MISSING CHILD

In Spanish, just as in English, there are two types of questions which can be formed: simple yes or no questions or interrogative questions which solicit more specific information. In English, questions can be very simple (only a few words) or they can be very complex. This is the case in Spanish as well.

In Spanish, there are words common to asking interrogative questions, and guess what, they are the same words used in the English language. Below are the most common interrogative words used to ask questions:

>Where?
>**¿Dónde?** *(dohn-deh)*

>When?
>**¿Cuándo?** *(koo-ahn-doh)*

Why?
¿Por qué? *(pohr kay)*

What?
¿Qué? *(kay)*

Who?
¿Quién? *(kee-ehn)*

How?
¿Cómo? *(koh-moh)*

How much/many?
¿Cuántos (as) / cuánto (s)?
(koo-ahn-tohs (ahs) /koo-ahn-toh (tohs)

Is/are there?
¿Hay? *(eye)*

Now let's talk about voice inflection and how important that is when asking a question. Take for example the following sentence in English: You have two children. As it stands, it is a statement. However, by adding a question mark to the end of the same sentence, it becomes a question. Notice that there is no difference in the words or the word placement. Now say these two sentences aloud. First, speak the sentence as if you are making a statement. Now speak the same sentence, making it into a question, by raising and lowering your voice (voice inflection).

Statement: You have two children (nearly monotone)

Question: YOU have two children? (stressing the "you")

The same grammatical principal applies to Spanish:

Statement: Usted tiene dos hijos.

Question: ¿*USTED* tiene dos hijos? (stressing the "usted") In English, as well as in Spanish, there are two types of questions – those that require information as a response and the basic "yes and no" types. Let's look at the **"yes and no"** type first. There are three ways to ask yes/no questions in Spanish.

1. ¿Juan come tacos? (formed by raising your voice)
John eats tacos?
2. ¿Come Juan tacos? (formed by placing the subject after the verb)
3. ¿Come tacos Juan? (formed by placing the subject at the end of the sentence)

This is probably an odd concept to learn at first. However, once you practice writing and then speaking various methods of simple yes/no questions, it will become easier.

Now, let's look at questions that are formed by **utilizing interrogative words**. Informational questions are formed by using an interrogative word, which is then followed by the verb of the sentence and then the subject of the sentence.

1. ¿Dónde quiere ir Ud.?
Where do you want to go?

Dónde – interrogative word
Quiere – verb
Ud. – subject

2. ¿Cuál es su dirección?
   Which is your address?

   Cuál – Interrogative word
   Es – verb
   Dirreción – subject

Now, let's talk a little about answering questions. Answering basic questions is made very easy by using nearly all of the words that were used in the question that was previously asked. Let's look at some examples:

1. ¿Come muchos tacos Juan?
   (Does) John eat a lot of tacos?

   Si, Juan come muchos tacos.
   Yes, John eats a lot of tacos.

2. ¿Cuántos hermanos tiene Juanita?
   How many brothers does Juanita have?

   Juanita tiene tres hermanos.
   Juanita has three brothers.

3. ¿Es famoso Pancho Villa en Mexico?
   Is Pancho Villa famous in Mexico?

   Si, Pancho Villa es famoso en Mexico.
   Yes, Pancho Villa is famous in Mexico.

MIRANDA WARNING

Spanish Translation

Antes de que hagamos cualquier pregunta, usted debe de comprender sus derechos:

1) Usted tiene el derecho de guardar el silencio.
2) Cualquier cosa que usted diga puede ser usada en su contra en un juzgado de leyes.
3) Usted tiene el derecho de hablar con un abogado para que el lo aconseje antes de que le hagamos alguna pregunta y de tenerlo presente con usted durante las preguntas.
4) Si usted no tiene el dinero para emplear a un abogado, se le proporcionar uno antes de que le hagamos alguna pregunta, si usted lo desea.
5) Si usted decide contestar nuestras preguntas ahora, sin tener a un abogado presente, siempre tendrá usted el derecho de dejar de contestar cuando guste. Usted tambien tiene el derecho de dejar de contestar cuando guste, hasta que pueda hablar con un abogado.

English Translation

Before we ask you any question. You must understand your rights:

1) You have the right to remain silent.
2) Whatever things you say can be used against you in a court of law.
3) You have the right to speak to an attorney so he/she can advise you before we ask you any questions and to have him/her present with you during the questions.
4) If you don't have money to hire an attorney, one will be appointed to you before we ask you any questions, if you do desire.
5) If you decide to answer our questions now, without having an attorney present, you always have the right to stop answering questions whenever you wish. You also have the right to stop answering questions until you can speak with an attorney.

NOTES:

ASSAULT AND DOMESTIC VIOLENCE

Did you call for help?	**¿Pidió nuestra ayuda?** *(peh-de-oh new-eh-strah ah-yuh-dah)*
Are you O.K.?	**¿Está bien?** *(eh-stah be-ehn)*
Do you need an ambulance?	**¿Necesita una ambulancia?** *(neh-sah-ceh-tah uh-nah ahm-buh-lahn-cia)*
What is your name/address?	**¿Cual es su nombre/dirección?** *(kuh-ahl ehs sue nohm-breh/deh-rehk-ceh-ohn)*
You need to go to the hospital.	**Necesita ir al hospital.** *(neh-sa-ceh-tah ear ahl ohs-peeh-tahl)*
Calm down.	**Cálmese.** *(kahl-mah-say)*
Tell me what happened.	**Dígame qué pasó.** *(deh-gah-meh kay pah-soh)*
Who did this?	**¿Quién hizo esto?** *(kehn eh-soh ehs-toh)*
What did they do to you?	**¿Qué le hicieron?** *(kahy leh eh-ce-herh-ohn)*
How many were there?	**¿Cuántos había?** *(kuh-ahn-tohs ah-beeh-ah)*
What direction did they go?	**¿En qúe dirección fueron?** *(ehn kehl deh-reck-ceh-ohn fuh-ehr-ohn)*

How long ago?	¿**Hace cuánto**? *(ah-say kuh-ahn-toh)*
How did it start?	¿**Cómo empezó**? *(koh-moh ehm-peh-soh)*
Where did it happen?	¿**Dónde le pasó**? *(dohn-deh leh pah-soh)*
Who started it?	¿**Quién lo empezó**? *(kehn loh ehm-peh-soh)*
He was / She was…	**Él estaba/ella estaba…** *(ehl ehstah-bah /eh-yah eh-stah-bah)*
Arguing	**Discutiendo** *(dihs-kuh-teh-ehn-doh)*
Taking drugs	**Tomando drogas** *(toh-mahn-doh droh-gahs)*
Drinking	**Tomando alcohol** *(toh-mahn-doh ahl-koh-ohl)*
Fighting	**Peleando** *(peh-leh-ahn-doh)*

Why were you fighting? ¿**Por qué estaba peleando**? *(pohr kay ehs-tah-bah peh-leh-ahn-doh)*

Children……………………..**Niños** *(nihn-yohs)*

Money…………………….**Dinero** *(deh-nehr-oh)*

Girlfriend…………………**Novia** *(noh-veh-ah)*

Boyfriend…………………**Novio** *(noh-veh-oh)*

Property..........................**Propiedad** *(proh-pee-eh-dahd)*

Drugs.............................**Drogas** *(droh-gahs)*

House............................**Casa** *(kah-sah)*

Drinking alcohol...............**Tomando alcohol** *(toh-mahn-doh ahl-koh-ohl)*

Questions relating to the assailant:

<u>**Tell me, did they.......to you?**</u>   <u>**Dígame, ¿Lo......*(deh-gah-meh, loh...)***</u>

Attack...........................**Atacaron?** *(ah-tah-cah-rohn)*

Bite..............................**Mordieron?** *(morh-deh-eh-rohn)*

Chase............................**Persiguieron?** *(pehr-see-geh-eh-rohn)*

Cut...............................**Cortaron?** *(korh-tah-rohn)*

Follow...........................**Siguieron?** *(see-geh-eh-rohn)*

Grab.............................**Agarraron?** *(ah-gah-rah-rohn)*

Kick.............................**Patearon?** *(pah-teh-ah-rohn)*

Punch............................**Golpearon?** *(gohl-peh-ah-ohn)*

Push.............................**Empujaron?** *(ehm-puh-hah-ohn)*

Rape.............................**Violaron?** *(vee-oh-lah-rohn)*

Rob....................**Robaron?** *(roh-bah-rohn)*

Shoot..................**Dispararon?** *(dis-pah-rah-rohn)*

Slap...................**Abofetearon?** *(ah-boh-feh-teo-ah-rohn)*

Stab...................**Apuñalaron** *(ah-puh-nyah-lah-rohn)*

Threaten...............**Amenazaron?** *(ah-meh-nah-sah-rohn)*

Touch..................**Tocaron?** *(toh-kah-rohn)*

Wound..................**Hirieron?** *(eh-reh-eh-rohn)*

Question pertaining to the physical description of the assailant:

Was it a man or woman? ¿**Fue un hombre o mujer**? *(fueh uhn ohm-breh oh muh-hehr)*

Was it a child, teen or adult? ¿**Fue un niño, adolescente o adulto**? *(fueh uhn neh-nyoh, ah-dohleh-cehn-the, oh ah-duhl-toh)*

Was the face covered? ¿**Estaba cubierta la cara**? *(eh-stah-bah kuh-bee-ehr-tah lah kah-rah)*

Can you tell me (about) **Puede dicerme**......*(puh-eh-deh deh-seer-meh)*

Race...................**La raza** *(lah rah-sah)*

Skin Color...................	**El color de piel**? *(ehl koh-lohr deh pee-ehl)*
Age...........................	**La edad**? *(lah eh-dahd)*
Weight........................	**El peso**? *(ehl peh-soh)*
Height........................	**La estatura**? *(lah eh-stah-too-rah)*
Hair Color...................	**El color de pelo** *(ehl koh-lohr deh peh-loh)*
Eye Color....................	**El color de los ojos** *(ehl koh-lohr deh lohs oh-hohs)*
Clothing.....................	**La ropa** *(lah roh-pah)*
Mustache.....................	**El bigote** *(ehl bee-goh-teh)*
Beard.........................	**La barba** *(lah barb-bah)*
Body Odor....................	**El olor del cuerpo** *(ehl oh-lohr dehl koo-ehr-poh)*

Describe (to me) the....	**Descríbame**....*(deh-screh-bah-meh)*
Attitude.....................	**La actitud** *(lah ahk-tee-tuhd)*
Complexion...................	**El cutis** *(ehl koo-teehs)*
Deformity....................	**La deformidad** *(lah dee-forh-meh-dahd)*
Freckles.....................	**Las pecas** *(lahs peh-kahs)*

Mannerisms......................**Los habitos** *(lohs ah-bee-tohs)*

Mark.............................**La marca / mancha** *(lah marh- kah / mahn-chah)*

Mole.............................**El lunar** *(ehl luh-nahr)*

Scar.............................**La cicatriz** *(lah see-kah-trehs)*

Smell............................**El olor** *(ehl oh-lohr)*

Speech...........................**El habla** *(ehl ah-blah)*

Tattoo...........................**El tatuaje** *(ehl tah-too-ah-hay)*

Voice............................**El voz** *(ehl vohs)*

Wart.............................**La verruga** *(lah vehr-ruh-gah)*

SEXUAL ASSAULT INVESTIGATIONS

VICTIM INTERVIEW QUESTIONS

Do you know the suspect?	**¿Conoce al sospechoso?** *(koh-noh-seh ahl sohs-peh-cho-soh)*
Describe the suspect.	**Describa al sospechoso/a** *(dehs-cree-bah ahl sohs-peh-cho-soh/sah)*
Victim........................	**Víctima** *(veek-tee-mah)*
Male/Female..................	**Hombre / Mujer** *(ohm-breh / moo-hehr)*

Height.........................**Altura** (*ahl-too-rah*)

Tall.............................**Alto/a** (*ahl-toh/tah*)

Short...........................**Bajo/a** (*bah-hoh/hah*)

Weight........................**Peso** (*peh-soh*)

Thin............................**Flaco/a** (*flah-koh / kah*)

Fat.............................**Gordo/a** (*gohr-doh/dah*)

Hair Color....................**Color de pelo** (*koh-lohr deh peh-loh*)

Blonde........................**Rubio/a** (*roo-bee-oh / ah*)

Dark Haired.................**Moreno/a** (*moh-reh-noh / nah*)

RedHaired...................**Pelirrojo/a**(*peh-lee-rroh-hoh / hah*)

Hair Length.................**Largo de pelo** (*lahr-goh deh peh-loh*)

Short Hair...................**Pelo corto** (*peh-loh kohr-toh*)

Long Hair....................**Pelo largo** (*peh-loh lahr-goh*)

Glasses.......................**Anteojos** (*ahn-teh-oh-hohs*)

Moustache...................**Bigote** *(bee-goh-teh)*

Beard..........................**Barba** (*bahr-bah*)

Hat.............................**Sombrero/Gorro**(*sohm-breh-roh, goh-rroh*)

Jewelry.......................**Joyas** (*hoh-yahs*)

Coat..........................**Abrigo** (*ah-bree-goh*)

Shirt..........................**Camisa** (*kah-mee-sah*)

Pants, Trousers................**Pantalones** (*pahn-tah-loh-nehs*)

Shoes.........................**Zapatos** (*sah-pah-tohs*)

Sneakers, Slippers.............**Zapatillas** (*sah-pah-tee-yahs*)

Scars.........................**Cicatrices** (*see-kah-tree-sehs*)

Tattoos.......................**Tatuajes** (*tah-too-ah-hehs*)

Deformities...................**Deformidades**(*deh-fohr-mee-dah-deh*s)

Firearms......................**Armas de fuego** (*ahr-mahs deh fooeh-goh*)

Weapons......................**Armas** (*ahr-mahs*)

Language.....................**Idioma** (*eh-dee-oh-mah*)

Do you know where he/she lives?	¿**Sabe dónde vive él/ella?** (*sah-beh dohn-deh vee-veh ehl / eh-yah*)
Are there any witnesses?	¿**Hay testigos?** (*eye tehs-tee-gohs*)
Are you hurt?	¿**Está herido/a?** (*ehs-tah eh-ree-doh/dah*)
Do you need an ambulance?	¿**Nesecita una ambulancia?** (*neh-seh-see-tah oo-nah ahm-boo-lahn-see-ah*)

Where did this happen?	**¿Dónde ocurrió esto?** (*dohn deh oh-koo-rree-oh ehs-toh*)
When did this happen?	**¿Cuándo ocurrió esto?** (*koo-ahn-doh oh-koo-rree-oh ehs-toh*)
Have you bathed?	**¿Se bañó?** (*seh bah-nyoh*)
What clothes were you wearing?	**¿Qué ropa llevaba?** (*keh rroh-pah yeh-vah-bah*)
Where is that clothing now?	**¿Dónde está esa ropa?** (*dohn-deh ehs-tah eh-sah rroh-pah*)
I will need to take these clothes for evidence.	**Necesito llevar esta ropa para evidencia.** (*neh-seh-see-toh yeh-vahr ehs-tah rroh-pah pah-rah eh-vee-dehn-see-ah*)
Where did he/she go?	**¿Adonde se fué él/ella?** (*ah-dohn-deh seh foo-eh ehl/eh-yah*)
What time did he/she leave?	**¿A que hora salió?** (*ah keh oh-rah sah-lee-oh*)
Did he/she leave on foot/ or in a car?	**Salió a pie o en auto?** (*sah-lee-oh ah pee-eh oh ehn ah-oo-toh*)
In what direction?	**¿En qué direción?** (*ehn keh dee-rehk-see-ohn*)
Describe the vehicle	**Describa el vehículo** (*dehs-cree-bah ehl veh-ee-koo-loh*)

PERSONAL INFORMATION

What is your name?   ¿**Cómo se llama?** *(koh-moh say yah-mah)*

What is your last name?   ¿**Cuál es su apellido?** *(koo-ahl ehs suh ah-peh-ee-doh)*

What is your complete name?   ¿**Cuál es su nombre completo?** *(koo-ahl ehs suh nohm-breh kohm-pleh-toh)*

Do you have a nickname?   ¿**Tiene un sobre nombre?** *(tee-ehn-ee uhn soo-breh nohm-breh)*

Another name?   ¿**Otro nombre?** *(oh-troh nohm-breh)*

What is your address?   ¿**Cuál es su dirección?** *(koo-ahl ehs suh dee-rehk-see-ohn)*

Name of the street?   ¿**Nombre de la calle?** *(nohm-breh day lah kyh-yah)*

What is your date of birth?   ¿**Cuál es su fecha de nacimiento?** *(koo-ahl ehs suh feh-chah day nah-see-mee-ehn-toh)*

Where were you born?   ¿**Dónde nació?** *(dohn-day nah-see-oh)*

Color of eyes?   ¿**Color de ojos?** *(koh-lohr day oh-hohs)*

Color of hair?	**¿Color de pelo?** *(koh-lohr day peh-loh)*
What is your social security number?	**¿Cuál es su número de seguro social?** *(koo-ahl ehs su new-meh-rroh day say-guh-rroh soo-see-ahl)*
What is your nationality?	**¿Cuál es su nacionalidad?** *(koo-ahl ehs suh nah-see-oh-nahl-ee-dahd)*
What is your marital status?	**¿Cuál es su estado civil?** *(koo-ahl ehs suh eh-stah-doh see-vehl)*
Single, married, divorced?	**¿Soltero, casado, divorciado?** *(sohl-teh-orh, kah-sah-doh, dee-vohr-see-ah-doh)*
How many children?	**¿Cuántos niños tiene?** *(koo-ahn-tohs neehn-yohs tee-ehn-eeh)*
Their names?	**¿Sus nombres?** *(suhs nohm-brehs)*
What is your father's complete name?	**¿Cuál es el nombre completo de su padre?** *(koo-ahl ehs ehl nohm-breh kohm-pleh-toh day suh pah-dreh)*

What is your mother's complete name?	¿Cuál es el nombre completo de su madre? *(koo-ahl ehs ehl nohm-breh kohm-pleh-toh day suh mah-dreh)*
What is your telephone number?	¿Cuál es su numero de teléfono - (home) (work) de su casa - de su trabajo? *(koo-ahl ehs ehl nuh-meh-roh day teh-lehf-oh-noh day suh kah-sah – day suh trah-bah-hoh)*
Employment: Name, address, and length?.	¿Empleo, nombre, dirección y cuánto tiempo en el trabajo? *(ehm-pleh-oh, nohm-breh, dee-rehk-see-yohn ee koo-ahn-toh tee-ehm-poh ehn ehl trah-bah-hah)*
How tall are you?	¿Cuánto mide usted? *(koo-ahn-toh mee-deh ooh-stehd)*
How much do you weigh?	¿Cuánto pesa usted? *(koo-ahn-toh pay-sah ooh-stehd)*
Do you have identification?	¿Tiene identificación? *(tee-ehn-eeh-ee-dehn-tee-fee-kah-see-ohn)*
Do you have a driver's license?	¿Tiene licencia de manejar un carro? *(tee ehn-eeh lee-sehn-see-ah day mah-neh-harh uhn kahr-rroh)*

Give me your driver's license, please. **Deme su licencia, por favor.** *(dehm-meh suh lee-sehn-see-ah, pohr fah-vohr)*

Have you been arrested before? **¿Ha sido arrestado?** *(ah see-doh ah-rrehs-tah-doh)*

What was the offense? **¿Cuál fue la ofensa?** *(koo-ahl fuu-eh lah oh-fehn-sah)*

    Abuse............................**Abuso** *(ah-boo-soh)*

    Allow.............................**Permitir** *(pehr-mee-teer)*

    Argue.............................**Reñir** *(reh-nyeer)*

    Assault...........................**Asalto** *(ah-sahl-toh)*

    Attempt..........................**Atentar** *(ah-tehn-tahr)*

    Beastiality......................**Bestialidad** *(behs-tee-ah-lee-dahd)*

    Bisexual.........................**Bisexual** *(bee-sex-oo-ahl)*

    Body Fluids....................**Fluídos del Cuerpo** *(floo-ee-dohs dehl koo-ehr-poh)*

    Body Odors....................**Olores del Cuerpo** *(oh-loh-rehs dehl koo-ehr-poh)*

    Breast (Chest)................**Seno (pecho)** *(seh-noh, peh-choh)*

    Burglary.........................**Robo** *(rroh-boh)*

Buttocks.........................**Nalgas** (*nahl-gahs*)

Burn.............................**Quemadura** (*keh-mah-doo-rah*)

Consent..........................**Consentimiento** (*kohn-sehn-tee-mee-ehn-toh*)

Copulation.......................**Copulación** (*koh-poo-lah-see-ohn*)

Conspire.........................**Conspirar** (*kohns-pee-rahr*)

Crime............................**Crimen** (*kree-mehn*)

Description......................**Descripción** (*dehs-krip-see-ohn*)

Fight............................**Luchar** (*loo-chahr*)

Gay..............................**Gay, joto** (male, slang) (*geh-ee, hoh-toh*)

Harassment.......................**Acosamiento** (*ah-koo-sah-mee-ehn-toh*)

Hit..............................**Golpear** (*gohl-peh-ahr*)

Homosexual.......................**Homosexual** (*oh-moh-ses-oo-ahl*)

Incest...........................**Incesto** (*een-sehs-toh*)

Injure...........................**Herir** (*eh-reer*)

Intercourse......................**Coito** (*koh-ee-toh*)

Kidnap...........................**Raptar** (*rahp-tahr*)

Kill..............................**Matar** (*mah-tahr*)

Know (person/place)............**Conocer** (*koh-noh-sehr*)

Lesbian.........................**Lesbiana** (*lehs-bee-ah-nah*)

Masturbate......................**Masturbarse** (*mahs-toor-bahr-seh*)

Nudity..........................**Desnudez** (*dehs-noo-dehs*)

Molestation.....................**Abuso sexual** (*ah-boo-soh sex-ooahl*)

Obscene Phone Call..............**Llamada obscena** (*yah-mah-dah ohb-seh-nah*)

Penis...........................**El pene** (*ehl peh-neh*)

Pervert.........................**Pervertido** (*pehr-vehr-tee-doh*)

Pornography.....................**Pornografia** (*pohr-noh-grah-fee-ah*)

Prostitution....................**Prostitución** (*prohs-teh-too-see-ohn*)

Rape............................**Violación** (*veh-oh-lah-see-ohn*)

Semen...........................**Semen** (*seh-mehn*)

Sodomy..........................**Sodomía** (*soh-doh-mee-ah*)

Solicitation....................**Solicitación** (*soh-lee-see-tah-see-o*hn)

Stab............................**Apuñalar** (*ah-poo-nyah-lahr*)

Torture............................**Torturar** (*tohr-too-rahr*)

Touch..............................**Tocar** (*toh-kahr*)

Transvestite.....................**Transvestista** (*trahns-vehs-tees-tah*)

Vagina............................**Vagina** (*vah-hee-nah*)

HOMICIDE INVESTIGATION

- Did you know the victim?

¿Conocía la víctima? *(kooh noh-see-ah lah vihk-tee-mah)*

- Do you know how the victim died?

¿Sabe cómo murió la víctima? *(sah-beeh koh-moh muhr-ee-oh lah vihk tee-mah)*

- Did you have anything to do with this death?

¿Tuvo algo que hacer con esta muerte? *(tuh-voh ahl-goh kay ah-cehr kohn ehs-tah moo-ehr-teh)*

- Was the death of this person due to self defense?

¿Fue la muerte de esta persona relacionada a defensa personal?
(foo-eh lah moo-ehr-teh day ehs-tah pehr-sohn-ah reeh-lah-see-oh-nah-dah ah day-fehn-sah pehr-soh-nahl)

- Do you suspect anyone?

¿Sospecha de alguien? *(sohs-pay-chah day ahl-gee-ehn)*

- Do you know if there are any witnesses?

¿Sabe usted si hay algúnos testigos? *(sah-beh oo-stehd see eye ahl-goo-nohs tehs-tee-gohs)*

- Do you own any guns?

¿Es usted el dueño de alguna pistola? *(ehs oo-stehd ehl doo-eeh-nee-yoh day ahl-goo-nah peeh-stoh-lah)*

- Do you own any knives?

¿Es usted el dueño de algúnos cuchillos? *(ehs oo-stehd ehl doo-eeh-nee-yoh day ahl-goo-nohs koo-chee-yohs)*

- Look at me when I ask you questions.

Míreme cuándo te hago preguntas. *(mehr-ee-meh koo-ahn-dooh teeh ah-goh preh-goohn-tahs)*

- Tell me the truth, do not lie to me.

Dígame la verdad no me mienta. *(dee-gah-meh lah vehr-dahd noh meeh mee-ehn-tah)*

- When did you last see the victim? Where? What time?

¿Cuándo fue la última vez que vió a la víctima? ¿Dónde? ¿A qué hora?
(koo-ahn-doh foo-eh lah uhl-tee-mah vehs kay vee-oh ah lah vihk-tee-ma? Dohn-deeh? Ah kay ohr-ah?)

- Who was with you when you last saw the victim?

¿Quién estaba con usted cuando vió a la víctima por última vez?
(keeh-ehn ehs-tah-bah kohn oo-stehd koo-anh-doh vee-oh ah lah vihk-tee-mah pohr uhl-tee-mah vehs)

- Who was with you when you last spoke with the victim?

¿Quién estaba con usted cuando habló con la víctima por última vez?
(keeh-ehn ehs-tah-bah kohn oo-stehd koo-ahn-doh ah-bloh kohn lah vihk-tee-mah pohr uhl-tee-mah vehs)

- Is there anyone who can verify what you are saying?

¿Hay alguien que pueda verificar lo que está diciendo?
(eye ahl-gee-ehn kay poo-eh-dah vehr-ee-fee-kahr loh kay ehs-tah dee-cee-ehn-doh)

- Did you touch the victim? Where? Why?

¿Tocó usted a la víctima? ¿Dónde? ¿Por qué?
(tooh-koh oo-stehd ah lah vihk-tee-mah. Dohn-deeh? Pohr-kay?)

- Were you mad at the victim?

¿Estaba enojado con la víctima?
(eh-stah-bah ehn-noh-hah-doh kohn lah vihk-tee-mah)

- Did the victim owe you anything? Money? Drugs?

¿Le debía algo la víctima? ¿Dinero? ¿Drogas?
(leh deh-bee-ah ahl-goh lah vihk-tee-mah. Dee-neh-rroh? Droh-gahs?)

- Were you jealous of the victim for any reason?

¿Estaba celoso(a) de la víctima por alguna razón?
(eh-stah-bah say-loh-soh/say-loh-sah day lah vihk-tee-mah pohr ahl-goo-nah rah-sohn)

- Did the victim do anything to anger you, your family or friends?

¿Hizo algo la víctima para enojar a usted, su familia, o amigos?
(eeh-soh ahl-goh lah vihk-tee-mah pah-rah eh-noh-hahr ah oo-stehd, suh fah-meel-ee-ah oh ah-meeh-gohs)

- Why do you think someone wanted to kill this person?

¿Por qué cree usted que alguien quisiera matar a esta persona?
(pohr kay kreeh oo-stehd kay ahl-gee-ehn keeh-cee-ehr-ah mah-tahr ah ehs-tah pehr-sohn-ah)

- How do you think the person responsible for this death should be punished? Why?

¿Cómo cree usted que la persona responsable por esta muerte debería ser castigada? ¿Por qué?
(koo-moh kreeh oo-stehd kay lah pehr-sohn-ah ray-spohn-sah-bleh pohr ehs-tah moo-ehr-the deeh-beh-ree-ah sehr kahs-tee-gah-dah? Pohr keeh?)

- Who else should I talk to about this death? Why? How can I contact this person?

¿Con quién más debería hablar sobre esta muerte? ¿Por qué? ¿Cómo puedo contactar con esta persona?
(kohn kee-ehn mahs deeh-beh-ree-ah ah-blahr soh-breeh ehs-tah moo-ehr-teh? Kooh-moh pooh-eh-doh kohn-tahk-tahr kohn ehs-tah pehr-sohn-ah?)

- Is there anything else you wish to tell me now?

¿Hay alguna otra cosa que quisiera decirme ahora?
(eye ahl-goo-nah oh-trah koh-sah keeh-cee-ehr-ah day-seahr-meh ah-ohr-ah)

NOTES:

MISSING CHILD

Calm down, please	**Cálmese, por favor** (*kahl-meh-say, pohr fah-vohr*)
Sit down	**Siéntese** (*see-ehn-teh-seeh*)
Slow down, please	**Despacio, por favor** (*dehs-pah-see-oh, pohr fah-vohr*)
Speak more slowly	**Hable más despacio** (*hah-bleh mahs dehs-pah-see-oh*)
What is your name?	**¿Como se llama Usted?** (*koh-moh seh yah-mah oos-tehd*)
Where do you live?	**¿Donde vive Usted?** (*dohn-deh vee-veh oos-tehd*)
What is your phone number?	**¿Cuál es su número de teléfono?** (*koo-ahl ehs suh nuh-meh-roh deh teh-leh-foh-noh*)
Are you the parent?	**¿Es usted el padre?** (*ehs oohs-tehd ehl pah-dreh*)
Are you the guardian?	**¿Es usted el guardián?** (*ehs oohs-tehd ehl goo-ahr-dee-ahn*)
Are you related?	**¿Es usted emparentado?** (*ehs oos-tehd ehm-pah-rehn-tah-doh*)

Who is missing?	**¿Quién está perdido?** (*kee-ehn ehs-tah pehr-dee-doh*)
What is that person's name?	**¿Cuál es su nombre?** (*koo-ahl ehs soo nohm-breh*)
How old is he/she?	**¿Cuantos años tiene?** (*koo-ahn-tohs ahn-yohs tee-eh-neh*)
What is his / her D.O.B.?	**¿Cual es su fecha de nacimiento?** (*koo-ahl ehs suh feh-chah deh nah-see-mee-ehn-toh*)
How tall is he/she?	**¿Cuanto mide?** (*koo-ahn-toh mee-deh*)
What color hair?	**¿Qué color de pelo?** (*keh koh-lohr deh peh-loh*)
What color of eyes?	**¿Qué color de ojos?** (*keh koh-lohr deh oh-hos*)
How much does he/she weigh?	**¿Cuánto pesa?** (*koo-ahn-toh peh-sah*)
What was he/she wearing?	**¿Qué ropa llevaba?** (*keh rroh-pah yeh-vah-bah*)
When was he/she last seen?	**¿Cuándo fue la última vez que lo vieron?** (*koo-ahn-doh fooh-eh lah uhl-tee-mah vehs keh loh vee-eh-ron*)
Where was he/she going?	**¿Adónde iba?** (*ah-dohn-deh ee-bah*)

In what direction?	¿**En qué dirección?** (*ehn keh dee-rehk-see-ohn*)
Was he/she alone?	¿**Estaba solo/sola?** (*ehs-tah-bah soh-loh/soh-lah*)
Are there health problems?	¿**Hay problemas de salud**? (*eye proh-bleh-mahs deh sah-loohd*)
Doctor's name?	¿**Nombre del doctor?** (*nohm-breh dehl dohk-tohr*)
Are there physical problems?	¿**Tiene problemas físicos?** (*tee-eh-neh proh-bleh-mahs fee-see-kohs*)
What language does he/she speak?	¿**Qué idioma habla?** (*keh ee-dee-oh-mah ah-blah*)
Names/addresses of friends	**Nombres/direcciónes de amigos** (*nohm-brehs/dee-rehk-see-ohn-ehs deh ah-mee-gohs*)
What school does he/she go to?	¿**A qué escuela va?** (*ah keh ehs-koo-eh-lah vah*)
Are there witnesses?	¿**Hay testigos?** (*eye tehs-tee-gohs*)
Were there any strange cars in the area?	¿**Había carros extraños en el área?** (*ah-bee-ah kah-rrohs ehs-trah-nyohs ehn ehl ah-reh-ah*)

Were there any strangers in the área?	¿Había desconocidos en el área? *(ah-bee-ah dehs-koh-noh-see-dohs ehn ehl ah-reh-ah)*
Any missing pets?	**¿Hay alguna mascota perdida también?** *(eye ahl-goo-nah mahs-koh-tah pehr-dee-dah tahm-bee-ehn)*
What kind of cat is it?	**¿Qué clase de gato es?** *(keh klah-seh deh gah-toh ehs)*
What type of dog is it?	**¿Qué clase de perro es?** *(keh klah-seh deh peh-rroh ehs)*
What is its name?	**¿Cómo se llama?** *(koh-moh seh yah-mah)*
Is the animal tame?	**¿Es manso?** *(ehs -mahn-soh)*
Is it mean?	**¿Es vicioso?** *(ehs vee-see-oh-soh)*
Does it have identification?	**¿Tiene identificación?** *(tee-ehn-neh ee-dehn-teh-fee-kah-see-ohn)*

NOTES:

CHAPTER NINE

INTAKE PROCESS / BOOKING PROCESS

MEDICAL INTAKE QUESTIONS

PROPERTY ITEMIZATION

➤ **Booking Form**   **Forma de arresto** *(fohr-mah deh ah-rrehs-toh)*

    Name: **Nombre (Completo)** *(nohm-breh (kohm-pleh-toh))*

    Address: **Dirección (Completa)** *(dee-rehk-see-ohn (kohm-pleh-tah))*

    City: **Ciudad** *(see-uh-dahd)*

    State: **Estado** *(ehs-tah-doh)*

    Country: **País** *(pah-eeys)*

    Telephone Number: **Número de Teléfono** *(nuh-meh-roh deh the-leh-foh-noh)*

    Date of Birth: **Fecha de Nacimiento** *(feh-chah deh nah-see-me-ehn-toh)*

    Race: **Raza** *(rah-sah)*

Nationality:	**Nacionalidad** *(nah-see-oh-nah-leeh-dahd)*
Sex:	**Sexo** *('sehk-soh)*
Age:	**Edad** *(eh-dahd)*
Height:	**Estatura** *(eh-stah-tu-rah)*
Weight:	**Peso** *(peh-soh)*
Hair Color:	**Color de Pelo** *(koh-lohr deh peh-loh)*
Eye Color:	**Color de los Ojos** *(koh-lohr deh lohs oh-hohs)*
Scars/Marks/Tattoos:	**Cicatrices/Manchas/Tatuajes** *(see-kah-treh-cehs/mahn-chahs/tah-too-ah-hehs)*
Show Me:	**Muéstreme los/las** *(muh-ehs-treh-meh lohs / lahs)*
Drivers License Number:	**Número de Licencia de Manejar** *(nuh-mehr-oh deh leh-sehn see-ah deh mah-nay-har)*
Social Security Number:	**Número de Seguro Social** *(nuh-mehr-oh seh-guh-roh soh-see-ahl)*
Custody Location:	**Lugar de Arresto** *(luh-gahr deh ah-rehs-toh)*
Place of Birth:	**Lugar de Nacimiento** *(luh-gahr deh nah-see-mee-ehn-toh)*

Employer's Name: **Nombre del Empleador/ Lugar de Trabajo** *(nohm-breh dehl ehm-play-ah-dohr / luh-gahr deh trah-bah-hoh)*

Work Address: **Dirección del Trabajo** *(de-rehk-see-yohn dehl trah-bah-hoh)*

Work Telephone Number: **Número de Teléfono del Trabajo** *(nuh-mehr-oh deh teh-leh-fohn-oh dehl trah-bah-hoh)*

Emergency contact/name and number **Nombre y número de teléfono de una persona en caso de emergencia.** *(nohm-breh eh nuh-mehr-oh deh teh-leh-fohn-oh deh uh-nah pehr-sohn-ah ehn kah-soh deh eh-mehr-hehn-see-ah)*

Who is this person? **¿Quíen es ésta persona?** *(key-ehn ehs ehs-tah pehr-sohn-ah?)*

Injuries/Illness **¿Heridas / Enfermedades?** *(eh-reeh-dahs/ehn-fehr-meh-dah-dehs?)*

Treated? **¿Atendido?** *(ah-tehn-de-doh)*

Treated by ..... **Atendido por......** *(ah-tehn-de-doh pohr...)*

Where Treated?	**¿Dónde le han dado tratamiento?** *(dohn-deh leh ahn dah-doh trah-tah-me-ehn-toh?)*
Date/Time Treated:	**¿Fecha del tratamiento?** *(feh-cha dehl trah-tah-me-ehn-toh?)*
Visible Injury:	**¿Heridas visibles?** *(ehr-ee-dahs vee-see-blehs?)*
Statute Number:	**Número de estatuto** *(nuh-meh-roh deh ehs-tah-tuh-toh)*
Ordinance Number:	**Número de estatuto** *(nuh-meh-roh deh ehs-tah-tuh-toh)*
Charge(s):	**Cargo / Cargos** *(kahr-goh / kahr-gohs)*
When were you interviewed?	**¿Cuándo fue entrevistado?** *(ku-ahn-doh fu-eh ehn-treh-vehs-tah-doh?)*
Warrant Number:	**Número de orden de arresto** *(nuh-meh-roh deh ohr-dehn deh ah-rehs-toh)*
Summons Number:	**Número de citación judicial** *(nuh-meh-roh deh see-tah-see-ohn hoo-deh-see-ahl)*
Vehicle Year:	**El año del vehículo** *(ehl ah-nyoh dehl veh-eh-kuh-loh)*

Vehicle Make:	**Marca del vehículo** *(mahr-kah dehl veh-eh-kuh-loh)*
Model:	**Modelo** *(moh-deh-loh)*
Style:	**Clase** *(klah-say)*
Color:	**Color** *(koh-lohr)*
Vehicle License Number:	**Número de las placas del vehículo** *(nuh-meh-roh deh lahs plah-kahs dehl veh-eh-kuh-loh)*
State:	**Estado** *(ehs-tah-doh)*
Location of Vehicle:	**Lugar donde se encuentra el vehículo** *(luh-gahr dohn-deh seh ehn-ku-ehn-trah ehl veh-eh-kuh-loh)*

> **Booking Area:**   **Área de Inscripción** *(ah-reh-ah deh ehn-scrip-see-ohn)*

You are at……	**Está en…** *(eh-stah ehn...)*
Stand here for your picture:	**Párese aquí para su foto** *(pah-reh-she ah-key pah-rah suh foh-toh)*
I am going to take your fingerprints:	**Voy a tomarle sus huellas digitales** *(voy ah toh-mahr-leh suhs way-yahs deh-he-tahl-lehs)*

Give me your hand:	**Déme su mano** *(deh-meh suh mah-noh)*
Hold your palms like this:	**Mantenga sus palmas de las manos así** *(mahn-tehn-gah suhs pahl-mahs deh lohs mah-nohs ah-see)*

> **Give me the....**   **Déme...** *(deh-meh)*

Thumb	**El dedo pulgar** *(ehl deh-doh puhl-gahr)*
Index Finger	**El dedo índice** *(ehl deh-doh ehn-dee-say)*
Left Hand	**La mano izquierda** *(lah mah-noh ee-kee-her-dah)*
Right Hand	**La mano derecha** *(lah mah-noh deh-reh-cha)*
Other one (hand or finger)	**La otra/el otro** *(lah oh-trah /ehl oh-troh)*
Clean yourself with this soap	**Límpiese con este jabón** *(lehm-pee-eh-say kohn ehs-teh hah-bohn)*
You have been arrested for....	**Ha sido arrestado por...** *(ah see-doh ah-rehs-tah-doh pohr...)*
Your bond is....	**Su fianza es...** *(sue feh-ahn-sah ehs...)*

The Bondsman are in the telephone book	**Los fiadores estan en la guía telefónica** *(lohs fee-ah-dohr-ehs eh-stahn ehn lah he-ah teh-leh-fohn-ee-kah)*
You can make three phone calls:	**Puede hacer tres llamadas** *(pu-eh-deh ah-cehr trehs yah-mah-dahs)*
Who are you calling?	**¿A quién está llamando?** *(ah key-ehn eh-stah yah-mahn-doh?)*
Do you want me to call?	**¿Quiere que yo llame?** *(key-eh-reh kay yoh yah-meh?)*
Tell them where you are now:	**Dígales dónde está ahora.** *(deh-gah-lehs dohn-deh eh-stah ah-ohr-ah)*
Sign here and keep a copy:	**Firme aquí y guarde esta copia** *(feer-meh ah-key ee gu-ahr-day eh-stah koh-pee-ah)*

JAIL BOOKING AREA

PROPERTY ITEMIZATION

> **Take off……..**   **Quítese…**(key-tah-say)

Bandana   **El pañuelo / La pañoleta** (ehl pah-nyuh-ehl-oh/lah pah-nyoh-leh-tah)

Ball cap   **La Gorra** (lah gohr-rah)

Bathing Suit   **El Traje de Baño** (ehl trah-hay deh bah-nyoh)

Belt   **El Cinturón** (ehl sehn-tu-rohn)

Blouse   **La Blusa** (lah bluh-sah)

Body Piercing   **Los Aretes del Cuerpo** (lohs ah–reh-tehs dehl kwehr-poh)

Book   **El Libro** (ehl leh-broh)

Boots   **Las Botas** (lahs boh-tahs)

Bra   **El Sostén** (ehl soh-then)

Bracelet   **El Brazalete** (ehl brah-sah-leh-tay)

Check (money)   **El Cheque** (ehl eheh-keh)

Cigarettes   **Los Cigarrillos** (loh see-gahr-ree-ohs)

Clothing	**La Ropa** *(lah roh-pah)*
Coins	**La Moneda** *(lah moh-neh-dah)*
Contacts (eye ware)	**Los Lentes de Contacto** *(lohs lehn-tehs deh kohn-tahk-tohs)*
Documents	**Los Documentos** *(lohs doh-kuh-mehn-tohs)*
Earrings	**Los Aretes** *(lohs ah-reh-tehs)*
Eye Glases	**Los Lentes (Anteojos)** *(lohs lehn-tehs (ahn-tee-oh-hos)*
Gloves	**Los Guantes** *(lohs gwah-tehs)*
Hat	**El Sombrero** *(ehl sohm-brehr-oh)*
Jacket	**La Chaqueta** *(lah chah-keh-tah)*
Jewelry	**Las Joyas** *(lahs hoy-ahs)*
Knife	**La Navaja** *(lah nah-vah-hah)*
Lighter	**El Encendedor** *(ehl ehn-sehn-deh-dohr)*
Matches	**Los Fósforos** *(lohs fohs-fohr-ohs)*
Magazine	**La Revista** *(lah reh-vehs-stah)*

Medicine	**La Medicina** *(lah meh-deh-sehn-nah)*
Money	**El Dinero** *(ehl de-nehr-oh)*
Nail Clippers	**El Cortaúñas** *(ehl kohr-tah-uhn-yahs)*
Necklace	**El Collar** *(ehl koh-yar)*
Overcoat	**El Abrigo** *(ehl ah-breh-goh)*
Pajamas	**La Pijama** *(lah pee-hahm-ah)*
Panties	**Las Bragas / calzones** *(lahs brah-gahs / kahl-sohn-ehs)*
Pants	**Los Pantalones** *(lohs pahn-tah-lohn-ehs)*
Papers	**Los Papeles** *(lohs pah-pehl-ehs)*
Purse	**La Bolsa/cartera** *(lah bohl-sah / kahr-tehr-ah)*
Raincoat	**El Impermeable** *(ehl eem-pehr-meh-ah-bleh)*
Rings	**Los Anillos** *(lohs ah-nee-yohs)*
Sandals	**Las Sandalias** *(lahs sahn-dahl-ee-ahs)*
Shirt	**La Camisa** *(lah kah-me-sah)*

Shoes	**Los Zapatos** *(lohs sah-pah-tohs)*
Shorts	**Los Patalones Cortos** *(lohs pahn-tah-lohn-ehs kohr-tos)*
Skirt	**La Falda** *(lah fahl-dah)*
Slip	**La Combinación** *(lah kohm-bee-nah-see-ohn)*
Slippers	**Las Zapatillas** *(lahs sah-pah-tee-yahs)*
Socks	**Las Medias** *(lahs meh-dee-ahs)*
Sport coat	**El Saco** *(ehl sah-koh)*
Sweater	**El Suéter** *(ehl sue-eh-tehr)*
Suit	**El Traje** *(ehl trah-hay)*
Sunglasses	**Las Gafas** *(lahs gah-fahs)*
Sweater	**El Suéter** *(ehl sweh-tehr)*
T-Shirt	**La Playera / Camiseta** *(lah plah-yehr-ah / kah-me-seh-tah)*
Tennis shoes	**Los Tenis** *(lohs tehn-eehs)*
Tobacco	**El Tabaco** *(ehl toh-bah-koh)*
Underwear (mens or womens)	**La Ropa Interior** *(lah roh-pah ehn-teh-ree-ohr)*

Unifom	**El Uniforme** *(ehl oo-nee-fohr-meh)*
Vest	**El Chaleco** *(ehl chah-leh-koh)*
Wallet	**La Cartera / Billetera** *(lah kahr-tehr-ah / beh-yah-tehr-ah)*
Watch	**El reloj** *(ehl reh-loh)*
Wig	**La Peluca** *(lah pee-luh-kah)*

ARREST COMMANDS

JAIL OR STREET AREA

Open your mouth and lift your tongue: **Abra la boca y levante su lengua** *(ah-brah lah boh-kah ee leh-vahn-teh suh lehn-gwah)*

Lift your arms: **Levante sus brazos** *(leh-vahn-teh suhs brah-sohs)*

Put your hands on your head: **Ponga sus manos en la cabeza** *(pohn-gah suhs mahn-ohs ehn lah kah-beh-sah)*

Put your hands on the wall: **Ponga sus manos en la pared** *(pohn-gah suhs mahn-ohs ehn lah pah-rehd)*

Put your hands in your back: **Ponga sus manos en la espalda** *(pohn-gah suhs mahn-ohs ehn lah ehs-pahl-dah)*

Interlace your fingers: **Entrelace sus dedos** *(ehn-treh-lah-say suhs deh-dohs)*

Show me the bottom of your feet: **Muéstreme sus plantas de los pies** *(mu-ehs-treh-meh suhs plahn-tahs deh lohs pee-ehs)*

Bend at your waist and spread your butt cheeks with your hands.

Dóblese y separe sus nalgas con sus manos. *(doh bleh seh ee seh parh-reh sus nalh-gahs kohn sus mah-nohs)*

INMATE RELEASE

Sign here please:

Firme aquí por favor *(fehr-meh ah-key pohr fah-vohr)*

This form shows that you have received your belongings:

Este formulario indica que usted ha recibido sus pertenencias *(ehs-tay fohr-muh-lahr-ee-oh ehn-dee-kah oohs-tehd ah reh-see-bee-doh suhs suhs pehr-tehn-ehn-see-ahs)*

This is the date you need to appear in court:

Está es la fecha que tiene que presentarse en la corte. *(eh-stah ehs lah feh-chah pah-rah kay preh-sehn-tahr-say ehn lah kohr-teh)*

This is where your vehicle is located:	**Aquí es donde está su carro.** *(ah-key ehs dohn-day eh-stah suh kahr-roh)*
Do you have all of your property now?	**¿Tiene Usted todas sus pertenencias ahora?** *(teh-ehn-eh oohs-tehd toh-dahs suhs pehr-tehn-ehn-see-ahs ah-ohr-ah?)*
This is your receipt:	**Este es su recibo** *(eh-steh ehs suh reh-see-boh)*
This is the name of your Probation officer:	**Este es el nombre del oficial que vigilará su libertad provisional** *(eh-steh ehs ehl nohm-breh dehl of-fee-see-ahl kay ve-he-lah-rah suh lee-behr-tahd proh-veehs-see-oh-nahl)*

QUESTIONS RELATING TO MEDICAL CONDITIONS

Do you have……?	**¿Tiene…….?** *(tee-ehn-ay)*
AIDS	**SIDA?** *(see-dah)*
Cancer	**Cáncer?** *(kahn-sahr)*
Chicken Pox	**Varicela?** *(vah-ree-seh-lah)*

Diabetes	**Diabetis?** *(de-ah-beh-tehs)*
Diptheria	**Difteria?** *(def-tehr-ee-ah)*
Epilepsy	**Epilepsia?** *(eh-pee-lehp-see-ah)*
Heart Disease	**Enfermedad del corazón?** *(ehn-fehr-meh-dahd dehl kohr-ah sohn)*
Hepatitis	**Hepatitis?** *(eh-pah-tee-tes)*
Leukemia	**Leucemia?** *(leh-uh-see-me-ah)*
Measles	**Sarampión?** *(sah-rahm-pee-yohn)*
Meningitis	**Meningitis?** *(mehn-ehn-he-tehs)*
Mumps	**Pulmonía?** *(puhl-mohn-ee-ah)*
Polio	**Polio?** *(poh-lee-oh)*
Tetanus	**Tétano?** *(teh-tahn-oh)*
Tuberculosis	**Tuberculosis?** *(too-behr-ku-loh-seas)*
Typhoid	**Fiebre tifoidea?** *(feh-breh tee-foh-ee-day-ah)*
Backache?	**Dolor de espalda?** *(doh-lohr deh eh-spahl-dah)*
Cold?	**Resfrio?** *(rehs-free-oh)*
Cough?	**Tos?** *(tohs)*

Fever?	**Fiebre?** *(feh-breh)*
Flu?	**Influenza?** *(ehn-flu-ehn-sah)*
Headache?	**Dolor de cabeza?** *(doh-lohr deh kah-beh-sah)*
Pain?	**Dolor?** *(doh-lohr)*
Sore Throat?	**Dolor de garganta?** *(doh-lohr deh garh-gahn-tah)*
Stomach ache?	**Dolor en el estómago?** *(doh-lohr ehn lah ehs-toh-mah-goh)*
Toothache?	**Dolor de muela?** *(doh-lohr deh moo-eh-lah)*
Is it contagious?	**Es contagioso?** *(ehs kohn-tah-he-oh-so)*
Is it infectious?	**Es infeccioso?** *(ehs ehn-fehk-see-oh-so)*
<u>**Are you………?**</u>	<u>**¿Está Usted……….?** **(ehs-stah oohs-tehd…)**</u>
Angry?	**Enojado/Bravo?** *(ehn-no-hah-doh/brah-voh)*
Anxious?	**Ansioso?** *(ahn-see-oh-so)*
Better?	**Mejor?** *(meh-hohr)*
Blind?	**Ciego?** *(see-eh-go)*
Calm?	**Calmado?** *(kahl-mah-doh)*

Comfortable?	**Cómodo?** *(koh-moh-doh)*
Confused?	**Confundido?** *(kohn-fuhn-dee-doh)*
Deaf?	**Sordo?** *(sohr-doh)*
Dehydrated?	**Deshidratado?** *(dehs-ee-drah-tah-doh)*
Disabled?	**Incapacitado?** *(ehn-kah-pah-see-tah-doh)*
Dizzy?	**Mareado?** *(mah-ree-ah-doh)*
Drunk?	**Borracho (a)?** *(bohr-'rah-choh (chah)*
Far-Sighted?	**Cegaton?** *(say-gah-tohn)*
Handicapped?	**Minusválido?** *(mehn-uhs-vah-lee-doh)*
Happy?	**Feliz?** *(feh-lehs)*
Hurt?	**Lastimado?** *(lah-steh-mah-doh)*
Injured?	**Herido?** *(eh-ree-doh)*
Irritated?	**Irritado?** *(irh-reh-tah-doh)*
Lost?	**Perdido?** *(pehr-dee-doh)*
Mute?	**Mudo?** *(muh-doh)*
Near-Sighted?	**Miope?** *(me-oh-pay)*

Nervous?	**Nervioso?** *(nehr-vee-oh-so)*
Numb?	**Adormecido?** *(ah-dohr-me-see-doh)*
Pregnant?	**Embarazada?** *(ehm-bah-rah-sah-dah)*
Sad?	**Triste?** *(tree-stay)*
Sick?	**Enfermo?** *(ehn-ferh-moh)*
Sore?	**Adolorido?** *(ah-doh-loh-ree-doh)*
Sweaty?	**Sudoroso?** *(su-doh-roh-soh)*
Tired?	**Cansado?** *(kahn-sah-doh)*
Uncomfortable?	**Incómodo?** *(ehn-koh-moh-doh)*
Upset?	**Molesto?** *(moh-lehs-toh)*
Weak?	**Débil?** *(day-behl)*
Worried?	**Preocupado?** *(preh-oh-kuh-pah-doh)*
Worse?	**Peor?** *(peh-ohr)*

Are you under a doctor's care?
¿Está bajo el cuidado de un doctor?
(eh-stah bah-ho ehl kwee-dah-doh deh uhn dohk-tohr)

Do you have heart problems?
¿Tiene problemas con su corazón?
(tee-ehn-eh proh-bleh-mahs kohn suh koh-rah-sohn)

Did you lose consciousness?
¿Perdió el conocimiento?
(pehr-dee-oh ehl koh-noh-see-me-ehn-toh)

Are you allergic?
¿Es alérgico?
(ehs ah-lehr-he-koh)

Are you taking medications?
¿Toma usted medicinas?
(toh-mah oohs-tehd meh-dee-seen-ahs)

How much do you drink?
¿Cuánto bebe usted?
(ku-ahn-toh beh-beh oohs-tehd)

HAVE FUN AT A SPANISH SPEAKING LOCATION FOR A MEAL

El Menú – The Menu

Carnitas – Pork

Carne molida – Ground Beef

Pollo - Chicken

Res – Beef

Bistec – Steak

Camanórnes - Shrimp

Mariscos - Seafood

Lechuga –Lettuce

Tomate – Tomato

Cebolla – Onion

Aguacate – Avocado

Queso – Cheese

Queso Fundido - Melted Cheese

Salsa – Sauce

Verde o Roja – Green or Red

Cubierta – Smothered

Relleno – Stuffed

Frijoles – Beans

Frijoles Refritos – Refried beans

Arroz – Rice

Caliente - Hot (temp)

Picoso (a) or **Picante** – Hot (spicy)

Tortillas de Harina o Maiz (Wheat or Corn)

La Sopa - Soup

Suave – Soft

Tostado (a) – Crispy

Tostadas – Chips

Miel – Honey

Azucar – Sugar

Sal – Salt

Pimienta – Pepper

Para Tomar? – Something to Drink (?)

Bebida – Beverage

Water – Agua

Té – Tea

Té Dulce – Sweet Tea

Soda (Dieta) – Soda (Diet)

Cerveza – Beer

Popote – Straw

Vaso – Glass (to drink from)

Hielo – Ice

Lemón – Lime or also known as: **Lemón verde**

Lima – Lemon

En la parte - On the side

Con – With

Sin – Without

Tengo hambre – I am hungry

Quisiera_____ - I would like _____

Quiero_____ - I would like_____

La Cuenta - The Bill/Check

La Propina - Tip

Mesero (a) – Waiter /Waitress

Plato – Plate or dish

Tazón – Bowl

Servilletas – Napkins

Tenedor - Fork

Cuchara - Spoon

Cuchillo - Knife

Gracias –Thank you

De Nada – You are welcome

Human Trafficking - Tráfico Humano

In this area of the book, I have placed basic questions concerning human trafficking. Please look in other sections of this book relating to obtaining personal information from the driver, passenger and those who were discovered as being trafficked.

What is your name? Date of Birth? Where do you live? Do you have any identification?

¿Cómo se llama? ¿Fecha de nacimiento? ¿De dónde vive? ¿Tiene alguna identificación?

(koh-moh say yah-mah? Feh-chah deh nah-see-me-ehn-toh? Deh dohn-day vee-veh? Tee-ehn-eh ahl-guh-nah ee-dehn-tee-fee-cah-see-ohn?)

What do you have inside of your vehicle/trailer?

¿Qué tiene dentro de su vehículo / remolque?

(kay tee-ehn-eh dehn-troh deh suh veh-ee-koo-loh / reh-mohl-keh)

Are there any hidden compartments?

¿Hay compartimentos ocultos?

(eye kohm-parh-tee-meehn-tohs oh-kuhl-tohs)

Do you know of anyone transporting humans illegally?

¿Sabe de alguien que transporta a los humanos ilegalmente?

(sah-beh deh ahl-gee-ehn keh trahns-porh-tah ah lohs uh-mahn-ohs ee-lee-gahl-mehn-teh)

Will you give me permission to search your vehicle/trailer?

¿Me dará permiso para registrar su vehículo / remolque?

(meh dah-rah pehr-meehs-oh pah-rah reh-he-strarh suh vee-ee-koo-loh / reh-mohl-keh)

Are there any weapons inside of this vehicle?

¿Hay armas dentro de este vehículo?

(eye ahrm-ahs dehn-troh day ehs-teh vee-ee-koo-loh)

Are there any drugs inside of this vehicle?

¿Hay algunas drogas dentro de este vehículo?

(eye ahl-guh-nahs droh-gahs dehn-troh deh ehs-teh veh-ee-koo-loh)

Is there anything that will hurt me if I search?

¿Hay algo que me haga daño si busco?

(eye ahl-goh kay meh ah-gah dahn-nyoh see buhs-koh)

Who are these people?

¿Quiénes son estas personas?

(kee-ehn-ehs sohn ehs-tahs pehr-sohn-ahs)

Where are they from?

¿De dónde son?

(deh dohn-deh sohn)

What are their names?

¿Cuáles son sus nombres?

(kuh-ahl-ehs sohn suhs nohm-brehs)

Where/what city did you place these people into your vehicle/trailer?

¿Dónde/qué ciudad se pogan a estas personas en su vehículo / remolque?

(dohn-deh/ kay see-uh-dahd say phn-gahn ah esh-tahs pehr-sohn-ahs ehn suh veh-ee-koo-loh / reh-mohl-keh)

Were you present when these people were placed into your vehicle / trailer?

¿Estaba usted presente cuando estas personas fueron colocadas en su vehículo / remolque?

(ehs-staba uh-stehd preh-sehn-teh kooh-ahn-doh eh-stahs pehr-sohn-ahs fuu-erh-ohn koh-loh-cah-dohs ehn suh vee-ee-koo-loh / reh-mohl-keh)

Who paid you to do this transportation?

¿Quién le pagó para hacer este transporte?

(kee-ehn leh pah-goh pah-rah ah-cehr ehs-teh trahns-pohr-teh)

Was the Mexican government/police or any other country a part of this illegal transport?

¿Fue el gobierno mexicano / policía mexicano o cualquier otro país parte de este transporte ilegal?

(fuh-eyh ehl goh-beh-her-noh meh-hih-kah-noh / poh-leh-ceh-ah oh koo-ahl-kee-her oh-troh pah-eehs pahr-teh deh ehs-teh trahns-porh-teh ee-lee-gahl)

How were you paid?

¿Cómo se pagaron?

(koh-moh say pah-gah-rohn)

How much were you paid to transport these people?

¿Cuánto le pagaron por transportar a esta gente?

(koo-ahn-toh leh pah-gah-rohn pohr tranhs-pohr-tahr uh ehs-tah hehn-tay)

Was this money paid in cash? From which country? From what person?

¿Se pagó este dinero en efectivo? ¿De qué país? ¿De qué persona?

(say pah-goh ehs-teh dee-neh-roh ehn ee-fehk-tee-voh) Day kay pah-eehs? Day kay perh-sohn-ah?)

Are these people a part of a cartel? If so, which cartel? Are you a part of a cartel?

¿Son estas personas parte de un cártel? Si es así, ¿qué cártel? ¿Es Usted parte de un cártel?

(sohn ehs-tahs pehr-sohn-ahs pahr-teh day uhn kar-tehl? See ehs ah-see, kay kar-tehl? Ehs uh-stehd pahr-teh day uhn kar-tehl?

Where are you taking these people?

¿Adónde llevan a esta gente?

(ah dohn-day yeh-vahn ah ehs-tah hehn-teeh)

Where did you enter into the United States of America?

¿Dónde entró a los Estados Unidos de América?

(dohn-day ehn-troh ah lohs eh-stah-dohs uh-neeh-dohs day ah-mehr-eh-kah)

Was anyone in the United States of America involved in this transport? Who?

¿Había alguien en los Estados Unidos de América involucrado en este transporte? ¿Quién?

(ah-bee-ah ahl-gee-ehn ehn lohs eh-stah-dohs uh-neeh-dohs day ah-mehr-eh-kah ehn-voh-luh-krah-doh ehn ehs-teh trahns-porh-teh)(Key-ehn)

How can I contact this person? Do you have a name?

¿Cómo puedo contactar a esta persona? ¿Tiene un nombre?

(koh-moh puh-eh-doh kohn-takh-tahr ah eh-stah perh-sohn-ah? Tee-ehn-eh uhn nohm-breh?)

Do you have a telephone number or address?

¿Tiene usted un número de teléfono o una dirección?

(Tee-ehn-eh uh-stehd uhn nuh-merh-oh day teh-leh-foh-noh oh uh-nah dee-rehk-cee-ohn)

How long have you been in contact with this person? Have you ever met this person? ; If so, where and when and how?

¿Cuánto tiempo llevas en contacto con esta persona? ¿Alguna vez conociste a esta persona?; Si es así, ¿dónde y cuándo y cómo?

(koo-ahn-toh tee-ehm-poh yee-vahs ehn kohn-tahk-toh kohn esh-tah pehr-sohn-ah? Ahl-guh-nah vehs koh-noh-see-steh ah ehs-tah pehr-sohn-ah. See ehs ah-see, dohn-day ee ku-ahn-doh ee koh-moh?)

Describe this person; Any vehicles? Did this person ever give you any money?

Describa a esta persona; ¿Algúnos vehículos? ¿Alguna vez esta persona le dio dinero?

(dehs-kree-bah ah ehs-tah pehr-sohn-ah. Ahl-goo-nohs vay-hee-kuh-lohs? Ahl-guhn-ah vehs ehs-tah pehr-sohn-ah lay dee-oh dee-nehr-oh?)

How was the money paid to you? Cash? Bank Transfer? Other?

¿Cómo se pagaron el dinero? ¿Efectivo? ¿Transferencia bancaria? ¿Otros?

Koh-moh say pah-gah-rohn ehl dee-nehr-oh? Eh-fehk-tee-voh? Trahns-fehr-ehn-see-ah bahn-kah-ree-ah? Oh-trohs?)

Are you an American citizen? If not, from what country?

¿Es ciudadano americano? Si no, ¿de qué país?

(Ehs see-uh-dah-dah-noh ah-mehr-ee-kahn-oh? See noh, day kay pah-ehs)

What routes do you use?

¿Qué rutas usa?

(kay ruh-tahs uh-sah)

Have you used these routes before?

¿Ha usado estas rutas antes?

(ah uh-sah-doh ehs-tahs ruh-tahs ahn-tehs)

Do you use a map? Telephone? Or GPS to find your routes?

¿Usa un mapa? ¿Teléfono? O GPS para encontrar sus rutas?

(uh-sah uhn mah-pah? teh-leh-foh-noh? Oh, GPS pah-rah ehn-kohn-trahr suhs ruh-tahs)

Who told you about these routes?

¿Quién se habló de estas rutas?

(kee-ehn say ah-bloh day ehs-tahs ruh-tahs)

Does anyone meet you when you are on a route?

¿Alguien se reúne con usted cuando usted está en una ruta?

(ahl-gee-ehn say reh-uh-neh kohn uh-stehd kuh-ahn-doh uh-stehd ehs-tah ehn uh-nah ruh-tah)

How many times have you transported people or drugs?

¿Cuántas veces ha transportado personas o drogas?

(koo-ahn-tahs veh-cehs ah trahns-pohr-tah-doh pehr-sohn-ahs oh droh-gahs)

Have you given food or water to these people?

¿Le ha dado comida o agua a esta gente?

(leh ah dah-doh koh-mee-dah oh ah-guh-ah ah ehs-tah hehn-teh)

NOTES:

INDEX

A

Accessories / Clothing, 90-93
Accent Marks, 16
Adjectives, 31-32
Advisement, Legal, 5
Answering Questions, 175-178
Alcohol Containers, 110-111
Alphabet, 11-13
Arrest Commands, 104-107
Articles (Grammar), 25-27
Asking for Documents, 100-102
Asking Questions, 175-178
Assailant Questions, 183-189
Assault Investigations, 183-189
Author Biography, 4

B

Biography / Author, 4
Body, Human, 76-79
Booking Terminology, 204-223
Byways / Streets, 102
Building Block –Defined, 37-47
Business Descriptions, 146-150

C

Car Descriptions, 116-117
Car, Felony Stop, 103-107
Car, Traffic Stop, 95-102
Cardinal Numbers, 74

Celebrations in Mexico, 157-160
Centimeter Conversion, 89
Chapter One, 11
Chapter Two, 70
Chapter Three, 87
Chapter Four, 90
Chapter Five, 95
Chapter Six, 129
Chapter Seven, 172
Chapter Eight, 175
Chapter Nine, 204
Child /Lost, 200-203
Clocks, 84-86
Clothes and Accessories, 90-93
Cognate Information, 68-69
Colors, 74-75
Commands /Arrest, 103-107, 115, 216-217
Commands / Jail, 208-218
Commercial Vehicle Inspection, 120-128
Compass / Directions, 88-89
Conjugate / How To, 36-68
Content Advisement, 5
Containers / Alcohol, 110-112
Crash Investigations, 117-119
Culture, 153-171

D

Danger Phrases, 129-138
Days of the Week, 87-88
Definite Articles, 25
Demonstrative Pronouns, 33
Diagram #1, 37
Diagram #2, 39
Diagram #3, 40
Diagram #4, 40
Diagram #5, 45

Diagram #6, 46
Diagram #7, 48
Diagram #8, 53
Diagram #9, 53
Diagram #10, 54
Diagram #11, 54
Diagram #12, 55
Diagram #13, 56
Diagram #14, 58
Diagram #15, 59
Diagram #16, 60
Diagram #17, 61
Diagram #18, 62
Diagram #19, 63
Diagram #20, 65
Directions, 88-89
Documents, Traffic Related, 96
Domestic Violence Investigations, 181-189
Driver Questions, 100-102
Drug Investigations, 143-145
Drug Street Slang, 139-141
DUI/DWI Information/Performance, 108-115

E

Emergencies, Traffic, 95-119
Expressions – Danger, 133-138

F

Family Defined, 160-161
Family Names, 165-171
Family Tree, 169-171
Features of this Book, 6
Felony Stops, 103-107
Food and Meals, 224-227
Forward, 5

Future Verb Tense, 64-68

G

Gender and Number (Nouns), 17-24
Grammar Concepts, 11

H

Height Measurements/Metric, 89
Hierarchy of the Latino Family, 160-161
Hispanic Culture, 153-171
Hispanic Definition, 154
Hispanic Family, 160-171
Hispanic Name Breakdown, 161
Holidays in Mexico, 155
Homicide Investigation, 196-199
Household Items, 150-152
Human Body, 76-79
Human Trafficking, 228-237

I

Indefinite Articles, 26-27
Infinitive Form of Verbs, 36-38
Injury Questions, 117-119
Inmate Release, 217-218
Inspection/Commercial Vehicles, 120-128
Intake Process, 204-217
Interview of Drivers, 95-96, 108-110, 117
Interview of Suspects, 181-193
Interview of Victims, 181-193
Interview of Witnesses, 181-193, 196-199
Investigation of Crashes, 117-119
Irregular Verbs, 52-63

J

Jail Booking, 204-223
Jewlery, 211-215

K

Kilogram Conversion, 89

L

Law Enforcement – Perception, 172-173
Legal Advisement, 5
Length Measurements/Metric, 89
Lost Child, 200-203

M

Marks on the Body, 90-94
Meals and Food, 224-227
Measurments, 88-89
Medical Questions, 117-119
Metric Conversion, 89
Miranda Warning, 179-180
Missing Child / Pet, 200-203
Months of the Year, 87-88

N

Names – Family, 165-167
Narcotics / Drug Slang, 139-141
Nationalities, 173-174
Nouns, 17-24
Numbers – Cardinal, 74
Numbers – Ordinal, 70-73
Number & Gender (Nouns/Adjectives), 17-24

O

Offices – Descriptions, 146-150
Open Containers, 110-112

P

Past Tense – Verbs, 56-63
Perception of Law Enforcement, 172-173
Performance Test / DUI, 113-115
Personal Information, 190-199
Personal Pronouns, 33-35
Pets – Missing/Lost, 200-203
Phonic Concepts, 15-16
Physical Descriptions, 184-192
Plural form of Nouns, 22-24
Prepositions, 27-30
Possessive Adjectives, 32-33
Poverty, 155
Present Verb Tense, 36-55
Preterite Verb Tense, 56-63
Pronouns – Demonstrative, 33
Pronouns – Personal, 33-35
Property Itemization, 211-215

Q

Questions, How to Ask, 175-178

R

Regular Verbs – Definition, 36-51
Religious Beliefs, 158-159
Religious Celebrations, 159

S

Scars on the Body, 93-94
Sex Crimes Investigations, 186-196
Singular form of Nouns, 17-22
Spanish Phonics Theory, 15-16
Spanish Sound System, 14-15
Stem of Verbs – Described, 37-38
Stops, Traffic, 95-115
Street / Byways, 102
Suspect Descriptions, 184-189

T

Table of Contents, 8-10
Tattoos, 93-94
Tenses –Future, 64-68
Tenses – Present, 36-55
Tenses – Preterite, 56-63
Time Expressions, 80-86
Time – How to Tell, 79-86
Traffic Crash Investigations, 117-119
Traffic Emergencies, 95-102
Traffic Stops, 95-102
Traffic Violations, 95-102
Trafficking – Human, 228-237
Types of Vehicles, 116-117
Tú – vs – Usted, 34-35

U

Undercover Drug Terms, 139-141
Undercover Drug Questions, 143-145
Usted – vs – Tú, 34-35

V

Vehicle – Commercial, 120-128
Vehicle – Descriptions, 116-117
Vehicle – Traffic Stops, 95-110
Vehicle Types, 116-117
Verbs – Irregular, 52-55
Verbs – Regular, 36-51
Victim Interview Questions, 181-193
Violations – Traffic, 95-102
Vowels, 14-15

W

Warning – Miranda, 179-180
Weapons, 129-132
Written Accent, 16-17
Weight Measurements/Metric, 89

X

Y

Z

A Road Officer's Guide – Second Edition

I sincerely appreciate your interest in making the Spanish language a tool in your law enforcement tool box. This book is the beginning to a new world of language skills. Please look for additional books relating to Spanish for all aspects of law enforcement that I will write. Please, practice – practice – practice!

If you would like to contact me, please go to: WWW.SLCSPANISH.COM., send an email or call. I look forward to hearing from my brothers and sisters.

<u>Stay safe and watch your six!</u>

Made in the USA
Columbia, SC
03 February 2020